June, 1980

Only The Beginning

Nelson L. Price

Dear Dean,
We hope you will
"live your life with a meaning
and purpose, living it to
the glory of God, for the
good of others, and with
respect for yourself."
Love,
Gram & Gramp

BROADMAN PRESS
Nashville, Tennessee

**DEDICATED to
Three sources of
inspiration—
My wife, Trudy, and
daughters, Lynn and Sharon**

All Scripture quotations marked NASB are from the *New American Standard Bible.* Copyright © The Lockman Foundation, 1960, 1962, 1963, 1971, 1972, 1973, 1975. Used by permission.

Verses marked TLB are taken from *The Living Bible.* Copyright © Tyndale House Publishers, Wheaton, Illinois, 1971. Used by permission.

All Scripture quotations marked RSV are from the Revised Standard Version of the Bible, copyrighted 1946, 1952, © 1971, 1973.

Dewey Decimal Classification: 248.83
Subject Heading: CHRISTIAN LIFE // YOUTH
Library of Congress Catalog Card Number:
Printed in the United State of America

CONTENTS

ABOUT NELSON L. PRICE

Maybe you have already met him. He speaks to over 100,000 youth a year, and multiplied thousands of them read his books, too.

He is the author of *Shadows We Run From, I've Got to Play on Their Court, How to Find Out Who You Are, Supreme Happiness,* and this book, *Only the Beginning.*

He is the pastor of the Roswell Street Baptist Church, Marietta, Georgia. He and his wife, Trudy, have two daughters, Lynn and Sharon.

INTRODUCTION

Congratulations! Welcome to the wonderful world of the graduate. This is a time of passing. You are moving from one stage to another.

It is a time for us to applaud you. Your achievement is noteworthy. Enjoy your hour. Savor your accomplishment. Take a deep breath. Acknowledge to yourself, "I did it!"

Solomon wisely wrote: "The desire accomplished is sweet to the soul" (Prov. 13:19).

Easy now, that's enough. Don't spend too much time reaching over your left shoulder with your right hand to pat yourself on the back.

It is hats off to the past
　　　　but
Coats off for the future.
　　This is—
ONLY THE BEGINNING.

Ralph Waldo Emerson logged these lines which remind us of this.

... there is one direction in which all space is open to us. Each of us has faculties silently inviting him in that direction to endless exertion. He is like a ship in a river; he runs against obstructions on every side but one. On that side all obstruction is taken away and he sweeps serenely over a deepening channel into an infinite sea.

Henry David Thoreau offered challenging insight.

"You have only to move in the direction of your dreams to meet with a success unexpected in common hours."

We must always relate to what *is*. To fail to dream of what might be would be to dehumanize ourselves.

In the fourth month of life within your mother, your heart suddenly began to beat. Someday, may it be distant, it will beat for the last time. Be sure that the life lived between those beats is lived with meaning and purpose. That involves living it to the glory of God, for the good of others, and with respect for yourself.

Charles Kettering once addressed an audience of engineers. He had a stage backdrop made of a massive sheet of stainless steel. It was perhaps thirty by fifty feet in size. Taking a metal stylus, he started at one corner of the sheet and made a tiny, almost invisible, mark across the sheet. He then explained that the mark he had made represented all that science had accomplished up to the present time. The large, polished, untouched expanse of the sheet represented what was yet to be discovered.

Though Kettering perhaps overstated humanity's accomplishments in science, his dramatization does indicate an opportunity. Mankind has left a lot of unmarked territory for you. Make your mark.

If you refuse to accept anything but the best in your quest, you are very likely to get just that—anything but your best!

In a life that is sure to end in death, don't ever play it safe:

Play it smart,
      play it wisely,
            play it intelligently.
Play it courageously,
      play it correctly,
            play it completely.

Play it for all it is worth,
        play it right,
                play it righteously.

Play it to the Lord. It solves the boredom problem.

In these days of your youth—your apprenticeship—it is more important to make yourself an effective instrument rather than to know exactly where and how the instrument is to be used. Be sure the metal is tempered, the blade sharpened, and then you can rest assured the world will use it.

An awkward, unattractive young Kentuckian once said, "I shall prepare myself and my opportunity *must* come." That young man was Abraham Lincoln. Opportunity knocked, Lincoln answered—*ready.* A tragedy of tragedies would have been an unprepared Lincoln. Don't let it happen to you. Live so you can look forward to remembering.

This is
        ONLY THE BEGINNING.

This is only the beginning. There is more change to come, so . . .

LOOK FORWARD

I've shut the door on Yesterday.
        Its sorrows and mistakes;
I've locked within its gloomy walls
        Past failures and heartaches.

And now I throw the key away
        To seek another room
And furnish it with hope and smiles,
        And every springtime bloom.

No thought shall enter this abode

That leaves a tarnishing stain,
And every malice and distrust
    Shall never therein reign.

I've shut the door on Yesterday
    And thrown my key away—
Tomorrow holds no doubt for me,
    Since I have found TODAY.

—Author Unknown

1. You Can't Go Back (Where You've Never Been)

Adam supposedly said to Eve as they walked out of the Garden of Eden: "My dear, we are living in changing times."

They were and so are we.

Change is inevitable. All progress and growth are a result of change. It is the only thing that has brought advance. Yet, the world hates change. There is nothing more permanent than change, and nothing meets with more resistance. Mankind has moved forward through the ages because man has had the intelligence to meet change with change.

"The survival of the fittest" has long been considered an ageless law of nature. Yet, "the fittest" are seldom the strongest. The fittest are those endowed with the quality of adaptation, the ability to accept the inevitable, to conform to the unavoidable, and to harmonize with existing and rapidly changing conditions.

There is great danger in reckless change. There is greater danger in blind refusal to change.

This is a time of tremendous change in your life. So far there has never been a time like it. This is only the beginning. Change is a way of life. It is important to use change as an occasion for improvement.

Certain moral and spiritual values never change, but circumstances and conditions never remain the same. It is necessary to establish the basis of understanding change.

This should be founded on unchanging Bible-based truth, which will help you interpret the changes just ahead and you can sail the stormiest sea.

One changeless factor is illustrated by a weather vane. A British pastor noticed a distinctive vane with the unusual inscription written under it—"God is love."

"Just what do you mean by putting that text there?" asked the minister. "Do you think God's love is changeable like that?"

"You don't get it," replied the farmer. "What I mean is, no matter which way the wind blows, God is still love."

There is a struggle for survival among ideas. Those ideas tend to prevail which correspond with the changing need of humanity. These are embodied in the Bible. An open mind may change with each new day, but the spirit and heart must remain as unchanged as the tides. The spirit and the heart must be governed by God's Word.

Many areas of your life will undergo change in a short time. Some phases to think about are:

Freedom

Before now the bounds of your freedom have been imposed by others. The outer limits of your "dos" and "don'ts" have been well-defined for you. You struggled to help define them. As a child you pulled at the control strings of your parents' patience to see what you could get away with. Gradually, you worked out your limits together. These boundaries have been flexible and have gradually changed with your maturity. But there probably has been parental veto power regarding your choices. They have had the ultimate ability to curb your activities. They have set time, place, person and activity boundaries. You have helped them but they have had the final say.

So many external restraints will be removed. Now your independence will require you to engage in self-discipline. *You alone* will be accountable for your conduct. There will always be the basic restrictions of society and institutions, but they are much broader than those. Not only are you free to choose—you are responsible for choosing.

Until now you have had little to do with making the major decisions that affect your life. That's about to change drastically. It's not only that you may now choose . . . you *must* choose. If you decide not to choose, you have in the nondecision chosen to let outside forces control you.

Previously, you have simply had to choose from a defined list of activities to engage in. Now you must determine the list and make the choices.

This new freedom is not the liberty to do as you please but the ability to do as you should. When what we want harmonizes with the Word of God there is peace and victory. Mental slavery exists when our desires conflict with God's nature.

Freedom requires decision. External pressures, put on you by superiors, must now be replaced by internal restraints. Your "someday" is *now*. You have longed for "someday" when you can make your own decisions. That moment has arrived. Don't discard the old limitations until you are confident that the new ones will be to the advantage of everyone involved.

Freedom requires discernment. Be sure that your freedom does not become just an opportunity for your lower nature. Bondage to your carnal self leads to suicide. This suicide may take one of four forms: mental, turning to drugs; moral, giving in to lusts; spiritual, resorting to the occult; or physical, actual self-destruction.

Freedom requires dedication. This is essential because now your decisions have lasting value and consequence.

Set your values and be sure they are yours. One of my daughters said to me, "I have reached the point where I want to do what I do, not because of who I am with, but because of who I am." That requires understanding of your true, best self and dedication to becoming that person.

Chances are that in this new-found freedom you can't live a straight A+ life. Expect some failures but do not accept any as defeats. Know that if you venture you may fail, but that does not mean you are a failure. There is a difference in the noun (failure) and adjective (failed).

Friends

Before now your friends have been prescribed by the limited circle you have lived in. Your immediate community, school, church, and family have offered a limited list to choose from. There has been a strong social, ethical, moral, ethnic, academic, and spiritual similarity among your friends. Your friends have been approved or disapproved of by your family. In many instances they have been long-lasting and always available. Time together has made them almost part of the family.

From now on you must choose your own friends. Many of your longtime, close friends will drift out of your life. Contact with many will be lost forever. Before their departure they will have influenced your life for a lifetime. Friends have a way of doing that. So it's very important that you choose the right new friends. They will almost instantly begin to influence your life. Be sure to choose wisely. You are not only choosing persons but *principles*. Their standards will bear influence on you. An overpowering friend can bring overwhelming influences to bear on you. In choosing friends, you are choosing a life-style.

Cultivate new friends. Emerson, commenting on our misplaced priorities, wrote: "We take care of our health; we lay up money, we make our roof tight, and our clothing sufficient; but who provides wisely that he shall not be wanting in the best property of all—friends?"

Reach out and touch somebody. Be a friend. He who would have friends must show himself friendly.

Jesus was a master of friendships. He placed importance on building caring relationships. He established close connections with those about him. He never did show a condescending attitude toward his disciples. Instead, he referred to them as friends and confided in them. He worked with them, talked with them, journeyed with them, and even refereed their intramural squabbles. As one follows Jesus through the pages of the New Testament, it is easy to see that he put great emphasis on friendship.

Work at making and maintaining good friendships. Recycle broken ones if possible. Samuel Johnson once said, "If a man does not make new acquaintances, as he advances through life, he will soon find himself left alone. A man, sir, should keep his friendships in constant repair."

If you develop a number of acquaintances, some of them are sure to hurt you. This is unfortunate but true. Isolation, though, is not self-defense; it is self-destruction. There are many examples that confirm an old Jewish saying, "He who goes far alone goes mad." Failure to develop friendships is failure to develop.

Friendship is the by-product of love. A wholesome love of self shows itself in a balanced love for others.

Teilhard de Chardin made a statement that we should think about: "Someday, after we have mastered the winds and the waves, the times and gravity, we will harness for God the energies of love, and then for the second time in the history of the world man will have discovered fire."

Let there be no energy shortage in your life. *Let love abound.*

When we lose a friend, we die a little. Stay alive—keep friendships alive.

Friends are not really made. They are recognized. That may be the principle problem of lonely people. They frequently fail to recognize the friendliness of those about them.

Be slow to give your friendship. When you have given it, strive to make it lasting. Don't make a person your friend until you have observed how he has used his former friends. Note that person's devotion to the Lord. A person who is not devoted to the loving Lord is not likely to be loyal to you.

Finance

Pregraduation, your world of finance may have been limited, but it has been predictable. Perhaps you began with an allowance. You might have thought it was given to afford you the ability to select what you desired. Actually, the purpose was to train you in the art of managing money. Others provided for you until you developed earning power. Likely your ability to earn has been restricted by time, age, and skills. In it all there has probably been a reassuring factor. You have known that if you got in trouble financially, more than likely a parent or guardian would come to your rescue. This has allowed for a little flexibility in money matters.

Now you are on your own much more. Now you must not only plan your own budget but provide the resources, at least in part. Smart money management will help you have peace of mind. It really does not matter how much you have. It is your attitude toward it and use of it that counts.

Resolve: Always strive to live within your means. Any person can spend more than he has. Only the wise person can live with *what* they have. Overspending can produce a bad credit record. It causes needless tension within and stress between persons. Reduce your wants rather than exceed your capacity.

Never borrow money needlessly. It is not good policy to borrow money to buy items that depreciate in value. If you must borrow, budget repayment in advance. If repayment will not fit your present income, do not borrow counting on an increase in income. If it does not come, difficulty will.

A person who does not pay back what he owes is described as wicked in Scripture: "The wicked borrows and does not pay back" (Ps. 37:21, NASB).

Avoid jeopardizing your reputation and freedom by improper debts. Solomon suggested the ultimate result of borrowing more than you can repay: "The rich rule over the poor, and the borrower becomes the lender's slave" (Prov. 22:7, NASB).

Limit your use of credit cards. Though they are convenient, they also encourage compulsive buying. As a general rule, those who can't pay cash, pay more. Shop for credit. There are different sources of credit and different rates of interest. "Plastic surgery" is often advisable— remove your credit cards when shopping if you tend to be a compulsive buyer.

We who profess to be free often become enslaved by debts. *Never seek credit when patience will allow you to make the same purchase later without paying additional interest.*

If youth but knew and age were able,
Poverty would be a fable.

Don't fall for get-rich-quick schemes. To earn and maintain wealth requires time, effort, and brains. A desire to make it "big" in a hurry indicates misplaced values. At two points the Bible speaks to this matter.

"He who makes haste to be rich will not go unpunished . . ." (Prov. 28:20, NASB).

"A man with an evil eye hastens after wealth, and does not know that want will come upon him" (Prov. 28:22, NASB).

Poverty and piety do not have to go together. There are numerous biblical and current examples of godly rich people. Integrity and/or inheritance is the surest road to financial success.

Don't allow yourself to be controlled by a compulsion to "keep up with the Joneses." Establish your financial position, and don't let pride force you out of it. Learn to rejoice with the Joneses. Never spend money you don't have on things you don't need to impress people you don't know.

J. Paul Getty was reportedly the richest man of his day. His statement regarding financial success not coming from keeping up with others is worth considering.

"The successful man," he noted, "must be very much of an individualist who can think and act independently."

Plan your budget. Make sure it is yours and not what is influenced and/or controlled by others. It will include such items as clothing, food, housing, insurance, entertainment, transportation, health, gifts, taxes, vacation, and education. Two items that should have priority are the tithe and a program of saving. Set aside sums for these purposes first. They provide for the Lord's work and your needs now— and in the future. Do not allow yourself to borrow from or delay payment of these items. Make them a priority.

In this matter and all matters, recall these words: "If you want favor with both God and man, and a reputation for good judgment and common sense, then trust the Lord completely; don't ever trust yourself. In everything you do, put God first, and he will direct you and crown your efforts with success" (Prov. 3: 4-6, TLB).

Framework

Before this moment your schedule has been dictated or controlled by authority figures such as parents and school officials. You have come and gone when and where they dictated. Little planning has been required on your behalf. This life-style hasn't given you a chance to project and select your schedule. Though such has been distasteful, it has sometimes afforded a degree of security. Watches and calendars have played only a small part in your life.

From now on, you become keeper of the calendar and of the watch. Budgeting of your time should always receive your maximum attention. If you don't plan your schedule, others will. Most often the others who will plan it neither know your interest nor best use of time. So, they dictate that which is least productive for you.

Yesterday's glory is ancient history. Past failures are to be forgotten. Don't live the life of a peacock whose glory is behind it.

Tomorrow is only potential. Don't waste today by worrying about tomorrow. Whatever you do, don't rush by today to get to tomorrow.

Make a daily list of your priorities and stick to them. A good time to do this is shortly before going to bed at night. If not, then do it the first thing in the morning. After planning it, commit it to the Lord as a schedule worth keeping, and have a good day.

In shaping your life-style framework, keep these things in mind.

Avoid fatigue. You can never do your best when physically, emotionally, or intellectually exhausted. Never hesitate to spend your last drop of energy in support of a worthy

17

cause, but in general keep fresh. This will allow you more energy for those special occasions that deserve your greatest energy. Maintain proper rest times.

Take care of your health. Poor physical health can affect all other areas of life. Regular medical check-ups are advisable, even for the young. Don't waste away your vitality. Proper diet and social habits influence health.

Take time to smell the roses. When possible, avoid stressful situations. If there is a prolonged period of stress, budget your time to relieve it through meditation and proper exercise. Never resort to unprescribed drugs to relieve stress.

Chart your mood. No person is ever as unlike other people as he that is unlike himself. Observe when you work best—morning, noon, or night. Match your biggest job with your best mood cycle. Chart emotional anniversaries and plan to bridge them with an adjusted attitude. The emotion of a past upset is often unconsciously relived when that time of year occurs. Be aware of moods.

Be mindful of the moods of others. Be sensitive to the changing moods and feelings of others. Adjust to needs for mood support in the lives of others. They also have pendulum periods. Watch the swing.

Shun situations that appeal to your impulsiveness. "Flee youthful lusts," was Paul's advice to young Timothy. Your own experience should have equipped you to recognize developing situations that tax self-discipline. If you're not going into a house, stay off the front porch. If certain conduct is out of character for you, don't flirt with the appeal.

Don't demand perfection of others, but strive for it in what you do. It is unfair to others and unjust to yourself if you require perfection. Do everything to the best of your ability and let that be the criterion for approval.

Strive for efficiency. Your desire should be to do a job well, not just fast. Evaluate the simplest, smartest, and least-exhausting way of doing a job. Work smarter, not harder. Don't use a shotgun to kill a fly or a fly swatter to hunt tigers. Match your resources with job requirements.

Assume your full responsibility. By this, I do not mean the kind a young man spoke of when asked if he were responsible. He replied, "Yes, I am. The last job I had, when anything went wrong they said I was responsible." Responsibility means dependability and reliability.

Be a thinker. When possible, deliberately think things through before making major decisions. If possible, write down the advantages and disadvantages. Try to avoid snap decisions. When possible, delay a day after making a major decision before carrying it out.

Establish a good motivational pattern for life. Then, when quick decisions have to be made, you will instinctively respond in the best way. A motivational pattern is established over a long period. You have worked on it all of your life. It simply refers to what motivates you. If you have a poor one, change it fast. Delay makes it even more difficult to change. Be sure you are not only highly motivated but properly motivated.

Accept lack of success as a learning experience. Never let failure defeat you. Learn from your losses. Look for ways of improving your performance and proficiency in each experience.

Rejoice always. In all things give thanks. There may be many occasions when you don't feel thankful. Feeling thankful is an emotional experience. Giving thanks is an act of the will. Develop the capacity of giving thanks. It will tend to lift you above despair. We are to give thanks "in," not "for" all things. This implies that not all situations are good, but in all situations your attitude and gratitude are good.

2. Never Climb a Tree
(Until You Get to It)

On a mantel in our home stands a beautiful, triple-cut chambered nautilus. A nautilus is a deep-sea mollusk. The chambered nautilus lives on the floor of the South Pacific and Indian oceans. The shell of the young nautilus is shaped like a small curved horn.

As the animal develops, the shell also grows. It begins to take on the shape of a spiral or coil. Each coil forms a new and larger chamber in which the nautilus lives. The nautilus moves forward into each new chamber and builds a wall behind itself. Each stage of growth is shown by a new chamber, which is closed at the rear.

The animal always lives in the outermost compartment of the shell. When a nautilus shell is dissected, each stage of growth is indicated by a chamber. Each outer chamber is larger than the one before it. Noting this, Oliver Wendell Holmes wrote:

> Build thee more stately mansions, O my soul,
> As the swift seasons roll!
> Leave thy low-vaulted past!
> Let each new temple, nobler than the last,
> Shut thee from heaven with a dome more vast,
> Till thou at length art free,
> Leaving thine outgrown shell by life's unresting sea!

Life has many chambers. Already you have occupied several. Before birth you occupied your mother's womb.

That was the smallest of chambers. The concentric chambers have developed rapidly. Preschool and elementary school days are chambers that have been vacated. Now your most roomy one to date, high school, is to become a sealed chamber. Soon it will be spoken of in the past tense.

Each in its time has been convenient. You have probably been comfortable. Movement from one to the other is always accompanied by unsettling uncertainty. Yet each has proven to be better than the last. Each has allowed for growth and development. The pain of passing from one to another is soon forgotten. The new stage with its expanded opportunities in no time becomes "the best—so far!"

Now confronting you is the challenge of building a "more stately mansion." Life's next stage will offer you a larger platform where you can act out this phase of life's drama.

No stage of our life is ever separated from all previous ones. As each is lived completely and constructively, it forms a part of the whole. There is no return to any past chamber. There is only the present one. The past is closed and the future not yet existent. Live in today's compartment so tomorrow's can be built with beauty.

Many uncertainties confront a graduating senior.

Shall I go to school or not? If I go, where should I go? If not, what should I do? Should I marry or shouldn't I? If so, whom and when? What career should I choose?

If you try to settle all of these weighty matters at once, it will be overcoming. Take them one at a time. Each affects the other. Do not borrow interest on tomorrow by worrying today. Never climb a tree until you get to it. Today has enough decisions to keep you constructively involved.

If the nautilus gets out of its shell, it becomes endangered by all sorts of sea predators that can destroy it. If we project unreasonably into the future with an agitated mind, we are plagued by anxiety, worry, and fear.

With faith in the living God, each new challenge can be confronted and conquered. A calm inexplainable confidence belongs to one who trusts God. This trust is spoken of by John Greenleaf Whittier in his poem, "The Eternal Goodness."

> I know not what the future hath
>   Of marvel or surprise,
> Assured along that life and death
>   His mercy underlies.
> And if my heart and flesh are weak
>   To bear an untried pain,
> The bruised reed He will not break,
>   But strengthen and sustain.
> And so beside the Silent Sea
>   I wait the muffled oar;
> No harm from Him can come to me
>   On Ocean or on shore.
> I know not where His islands lift
>   Their fronded palms in air;
> I only know I cannot drift
>   Beyond His love and care.

The inaudible voice and unfelt hand are available to guide those who desire His help.

Joshua was a splendid leader who lived much of his life in the shadow of a giant among men, Moses. Joshua greatly admired Moses. At the death of Moses, Joshua emerged in a new stage of his own growth. Heroes die, but the power that produces them lives on. The reasons for Joshua's development, when revealed, can help others grow. Underlying his emerging success was a belief in a promise God made to him (which is applicable to each of us).

"This book of the law shall not depart out of thy mouth; but thou shalt meditate therein day and night, that thou mayest observe to do according to all that is written therein: for then thou shalt make thy way prosperous, and then thou shalt have good success. Have not I commanded thee? Be strong and of a good courage; be not afraid, neither be thou dismayed: for the Lord thy God is with thee whithersoever thou goest" (Josh. 1:8,9).

First, he had the right . . .

Internal Attitude

He had strength and showed courage. So, he possessed the Promised Land.

There were two vital contributors to the strength of Joshua. One was persistence. He had been an Egyptian slave for forty years. For four decades he lived in one of life's cramped chambers—the chamber of bondage. Next he wandered for forty years in the wilderness. Patiently and persistently he did his best in each stage of development. And when the time of his emergence arrived, he was prepared and ready.

The aloe plant blooms once every 100 years. Some of life's beauty can be produced only at the price of time. A mushroom can emerge overnight, but years are required, even centuries, to produce the stately cypress tree.

I once commented to a college coach that his high-school-age son had a potentially bright future. He remarked, "Yes he does. If we can just convince him that not all good things in life are on this side of the hill." Save some of life for tomorrow. Energetically invest yourself in the best today so tomorrow's treasures can be tapped through persistence.

Give even the smallest invitation a great response. Then, you can be assured of other and better invitations.

Stick-to-it-ness is still a valuable virtue. Jesus Christ worked almost unknown for thirty years before his public ministry began.

A sense of purpose also contributed to the strength of Joshua. Though Joshua was sensitive of his inabilities, he was also aware of a sense of "calling." He had a purpose. Being conscious of his lack of ability, he relied on the Lord. Never be so self-sufficient that you cannot be used. One might well be concerned about failing the Lord were it not for an awareness that He will never fail us. Persistence and a sense of purpose give strength today as it did for Joshua.

The strength of Joshua stimulated his courage. His reason for courage was the promise "I will be with thee." God so greatly admires courage that he makes himself the constant companion of the courageous.

Joshua was advised not to be "afraid or dismayed." When God said "be not afraid," it was always an indication someone was afraid. When he instructed someone to be strong, it was because that person was weak. Joshua was.

Never let your fears dominate. Fear exaggerates difficulties—murmurs at duty—shrinks from reproach— postpones duty, then neglects it, then hates God with bitterness and despair. Ultimately, it weakens its host to the point of abject despair. It devours lives. It is the enemy of ambition.

Rudyard Kipling wisely wrote of fear: "Of all the liars of the world, sometimes the worst are your own fears."

Adam and Eve were afraid and hid themselves. The servant given one talent was afraid and hid his talent.

The word courage refers not only to attitude but action. It means being vigorous, alert, prompt, and ready to serve with enthusiasm. Every job is a self-portrait of the doer. Autograph your work with excellence.

The momentum of a projectile (bullet), is the product of

its mass (size) and velocity (speed). A lighter ball driven by a greater force will do more work than a heavier one driven by less force. This physical principle is also true in the realm of personal productivity. Often less-talented persons accomplish and achieve more than those more gifted. Courage is one's force. It can compensate for size, talent, ability, and capacity. If one is vigorous, alert, prompt, and ready to serve with enthusiasm, much can be accomplished.

Joshua also engaged in the right . . .

External Action

He meditated on the right things and was obedient to do them. Meditation takes place in the realm of the mind. Bible-based meditation helps a person to remember his origin and enables the heart to lose itself in God. Keep the ever-flowing stream of your mind fresh. Soak yourself in the best attitudes. It is really not as difficult as to let the mind marinate in cheap and tarnished things.

Many meditate on mediocrity and are not ashamed of it. Your thoughts are your constant companions. They can be chosen from the most exciting minds on earth. This can be done through the magic of the written word. Reading inspiring, uplifting things can help you achieve the fullest.

The apostle Paul wisely listed an inventory of ideals in Phillippians 4:8: "Finally, brethren, whatsoever things are true, whatsoever things are honest, whatsoever things are just, whatsoever things are pure, whatsoever things are lovely, whatsoever things are of good report; if there be any virtue, and if there be any praise, think on these things."

Incorporate in your daily schedule a time for reading and thinking on a Bible passage. An ambassador who refuses to open a letter of instruction from his president, and pleads innocence on the basis of not knowing his orders, would plead in vain. The very innocence he would plead would be a confession of another guilt.

The doing of God's work is the most sure way to peace and happiness. To do His work one must know His will. To know his will one must know his Word. Hide his words in your heart that you might not sin against him (Ps. 119:11).

We are not only responsible for doing what we know, but for knowing what we may do.

Not only did Joshua meditate on the right thoughts, he also engaged in the right tasks. He "observed to do" God's will. A lack of obedience shows lax faith. This expresses a loss of trust.

To do God's will means to act skillfully. So a skilled workman is one doing the will of God.

Joshua's internal attitude and external action were based on . . .

Eternal Axioms

In agriculture there are certain processes that will produce the goods. In banking there are principles that work. In ecology, as well as economy, certain specific rules work. In the realm of the spirit there are also distinctive principles that have a predictable result.

It is still true —
> We reap what we sow.
> > We reap more than we sow.
> > > We reap later than we sow.

The person who steers by God's chart and compass is prevented from running aground on jagged rocks. Such a person is most likely to reach his desired goals.

An axiom is a recognized truth. Certain basic truths should be filed in your memory bank to pay dividends as needed. Some are:

Axiom One—Have an invisible means of support.

Though there are times we may seem to be alone, we are not. On Christmas Eve, 1944, Martin Niemoeller was a prisoner in Hitler's Dachau concentration camp. Amid that horror, which could have caused him to lose his mind, he wrote:

> We are not alone amidst the horror of these years, cut-off though we are from the outside world. We are in the Hands of God. . . . He is with us in this dismal and lonely place to hold and comfort us and keep hope alive in our hearts.

Friends may forsake us. Circumstances may plot against us. Hope may be faint but we are never alone in our hour of need. Some see only a hopeless end, but the Christian rejoices in an endless hope. There is an *invisible* means of support available.

Even when we do not feel God's presence, he is there. Poor digestion, loss of sleep, a quarrel with a friend, or such a simple thing as room temperature may cause us to feel dejected. This may lead us not to sense God's presence. Feeling is only one antenna. Fact is another more reliable one. The fact is: He said: "I will never leave you . . . I will be with you always . . ." He is Immanuel—God with us.

Axiom Two—God is a merciful God. There are many things which are difficult to understand in this life. Many puzzles seem to have no solution. Riddles without answers abound. The loose end of some of life's most knotty issues is God's mercy. Governor Bradford of the Plymouth Colony wrote ageless truth in his journal during a crisis time:

> Our fathers came over this ocean and were ready to perish in this wilderness but they cried out unto the Lord and He heard their voices and had mercy on their adversities. Let us, therefore, praise Him because Hie is good and His mercies endure forever.

Even when the times are not good, God is. Goodness is a part of his unchanging nature. God is good because he is a good God.

Axiom Three—Each moment of life is a time of testing or temptation. Our responses are much more important than our circumstances. A trial gives us an opportunity to stand faithful to our convictions. A temptation gives occasion for our weaknesses to be exploited.

In the great epic, "The Odyssey," the poet Homer tells how the Greek general, Ulysses, was leading his army toward Troy. Unexpectedly, they came upon a flooded river that his men could not cross. He was so frustrated by this that he waded out into the waters up to his knees. There he vented his fury by thrashing the water with chains. Needless to say, it was to no avail. This is a graphic image of how some people respond to difficulty.

If, as in the words of the old hymn, "I Won't Have to Cross Jordan Alone," surely there is no need to thrash at the troublesome waters of life.

Another writing with its background in Greece reveals a more stable option. The city of Corinth, established in 800, was the setting for an encounter. The apostle Paul was a bold leader and great thinker. There he was confronted with the threat of death. Courageously, he stood on the Rostra overlooking the Agora and spoke to his taunters.

This man, whose intellect was not exceeded by Aristotle, Plato, or Socrates, confounded his enemies who would be his executioners. He said, "For this slight momentary affliction is preparing for us an eternal weight of glory beyond all comparison" (2 Cor. 4:17, RSV). He was saying that death is not the end of life, but a part of it.

Don't let the circumstances of life master you—you master them. It is not thrashing chains but trusting faith that enables one to succeed.

Axiom Four—Do not waste time. Ben Franklin called it "the substance life is made of." Philip Dormer Stanhope, the Earl of Chesterfield, penned this wisdom: "Know the true value of time. Snatch it, seize it, enjoy every second of it. No laziness, no idleness, no procrastination; never put off until tomorrow what you can do today."

In ancient Sanskrit, the following was recorded:

Look well to this one day, for it, and it alone, is life. In the brief course of this one day, lie all the verities and realities of your existence; the pride of growth, the glory of action, the splendor of beauty. Yesterday is but a dream and tomorrow a vision. Yet, each day, well-lived, makes every yesterday a dream of happiness and each tomorrow a vision of hope. Look well, therefore, to this one day, for it, and it alone is life.

Yesterday is gone and tomorrow is not guaranteed. So make today your day. Make it the best day of your life—so far. Be kind to your tomorrow self. Your today self's actions are being filed away as memories. Approach each day with the attitude, "I'm going to make a memory."

Axiom Five—To live one must grow. Personal development usually falls into one or two categories—wasp or crocodile.

A wasp is as large on the day it is hatched as it will ever be. A crocodile keeps on growing right up to the day it dies.

Which are you?

For some, graduation is a time of hatching. Some are as big as they will ever be. Their education is complete. That milestone marks the maximum of their "waspish" development.

Other people keep on growing. Life continues to be an exciting adventure. They are constantly confronting the challenges of new horizons. Growth is a way of life for these "crocodiles."

Growth should have four facets: Social, physical, mental, and spiritual. Do not neglect any. The perfectly balanced life of Jesus Christ was described by Luke as follows: "And Jesus increased in wisdom (mentally) and stature (physically), and in favour with God (spiritually) and man (socially)" (Luke 2:52). Jesus is a matchless model.

When Joshua came to the borders of the Land of Promise he shared the following counsel with his followers (and applicable to every graduate): ". . . that ye may know the way by which ye must go: for ye have not passed this way heretofore" (Josh. 3:4b).

Fortunately for graduates, others have walked the paths before them. This past enables a person to learn experientially or academically. One can learn experientially that a hot stove will burn *by touching it.* Another could learn the same lesson by *talking to a person who has touched one, or by reading* in a medical journal the effect of touching a hot stove.

Experience is not the only teacher in life. Experience is a good educator, but the fees are often expensive. Learn the axioms inherited from those who have walked the path before you.

Walk as one who is done with fear
Knowing that the God of love is near.
Live each day in such a way that you can
Look forward to remembering.

3. Back to the Basics

"Stand by! Ready! Action."

That's your cue. It's time for you to step on to the stage and play your role in life. It is a big cast. Be careful; don't get lost in the shuffle. The struggle is about to begin. Don't kid yourself; it *is* going to be a struggle. It has been for every other actor on this stage, so don't expect to be an exception.

Every scene is for real. There is no rerun. Do your lines right the first time; there are no retakes.

Be sure to put on the right makeup. Take the mirror of your mind in hand and check to see that you are properly costumed for the role you are to play. You have cast yourself. What is it? Clown or contributor? How will you play it? Cowering or confident?

Some look into the mirror and see themselves as failures. They always have. Maybe they first developed this image from hearing parents parrot it. Perhaps a few circumstances caused major setbacks, and the role was chosen. Such characters in life's saga cower from their role for fear of further failure. So they spend a lifetime expecting defeat and never trying to achieve. Actually, they never expect to accomplish anything. They have dictated to themselves a character that can't achieve. Success would be out of character for them. They have no self-trust.

Others look in the mirror and see themselves as confident doers. They have spent time in makeup getting ready for the role. They work to achieve because they are confident that they can obtain their goals. Struggle, defeat, and criticism have also played a part in their lives. They have been motivated by them. A greater resolve has resulted from setbacks. They have not been blind to their successes, achievements, and attainments. They hunger for more of the same. Driven by this noble desire they are confident.

Now is the time to dig out your buried treasure and look at it. Show it to the world. Don't let false modesty cause you to keep it hidden. Confidence. That is your internal treasure. It can help you develop or renew your sense of what you *can be* in life or what you *can do.*

It's not too late to let it mature. The very fact that you have had failures but are now going to demonstrate confidence indicates you have the capacity. Failures as well as successes can lead to more of the same—or the opposite. It is simply a matter of your response to them. Others have failed and come on strong.

Walt Disney was released from his first major newspaper job because he "had little talent as an artist."

Albert Einstein was thought of as a mediocre student by his grade-school teachers. In fact, one of them called him a "dummkopf" (blockhead).

Napoleon Bonaparte had the dubious distinction of graduating 42nd in his military class of 43.

Thomas Edison had so much difficulty in school that his father feared Tom was stupid.

Louis Pasteur was written off by his teacher as ". . . the meekest, smallest, and least promising student in my class."

They all had numerous, significant losses, but one thing they never lost was confidence.

Belief in a loving God is the most important belief in life. Second only to this is belief in yourself. Self-trust is the first secret to success. If you can't trust the Lord and you won't trust yourself, who and what can you trust? The alternative leaves you with a suspicious, fearful life.

Know your limit and then go your limit. If you have just squeezed through high school science, don't plan to be a doctor. If you are five feet two, don't plan to play in the National Basketball Association.

Everyone has limits. Don't be embarrassed or discouraged because you do. Identify them. Be careful; don't be too negative. Identify your maximum limits. What do you think you can be and do if you extend yourself and use your full potential? Don't consider what others have suggested you can and can't do. Don't make this judgment on the basis of what you have done. If you really apply yourself, what you really *deep down* know you can do . . . do it!

Don't fail because you won't try for fear of failure. Don't fail because you have failed and are fearful of failing. Believe in yourself. Extend yourself. Depend on yourself. Exert yourself. Develop yourself.

Some persons feel guilty when they feel confident. They think others are destined to succeed, but they are only worthy of failure. If they achieve they are almost apologetic. "Somebody else deserves success—not me," is their outlook. This kind of person looks on his successes as "luck." He feels sure it won't happen again. It was just a break.

Shed that garment of self-deception. You are a person deserving of the best—your best. Confidently re-evaluate what your best really is. Forget about what it has been. Think about what it can be. Redefine your upper limits—confidently.

The eighteenth-century British statesman, Edmund Burke, wisely said, "Those things which are not practicable are not desirable. There is nothing in the world really beneficial that does not lie within the reach of an informed understanding and well-directed pursuit." .

Since that's true, you can be a confident doer. Decide

what you know to be really beneficial. Become informed. Direct your energies. You might even amaze yourself.

The following are some confidence-developing exercises.

Discard the negative. Flush your mind of stale defeatist attitudes. Storm the castle of your thoughts. Drive out the would-be tyrant, "failure." Recapture your mind. Let positive principles control.

There is no such thing as idle thoughts. All your thinking works either for good or bad. Positive thought can make you stronger. Negative thought is exhausting.

Think with your mind, not your hopes, fears, or wishes. Employ your reason and use logic.

In his younger days, the late French statesman George Clemenceau fought a number of duels. One of these was to be fought in a suburb of Paris. His "second" went with him to the railway station and observed as George bought a one-way ticket.

"A one-way ticket?" said the second. "Pessimistic?"

"Not at all," said Clemenceau cheerfully. "I always use my opponent's return ticket for the trip back."

With confidence like that, it is little wonder that Clemenceau was successful.

No person can live long without realizing that life deals some losses, defeats, and disappointments to everyone. The optimist is not blind to this reality. He is fully aware of this and is prepared to accept his share of the bad. It is simply that he is resolute in recovering the good and later using the lessons learned to gain other victories.

Such a person positively accepts the fact that in everything which happens God is busy bringing the good out of it. If God is so inclined, it's a good attitude for us. This truth gives confidence resulting in rejoicing in all things.

Define realistic goals. What do you want out of life—

34

not what you can get, but what you can be. Be practical, but be positive. Establish what you want.

The difference that Jesus Christ made in human affairs was not that he said, "You must," more sternly than anyone, but that he said, "With me, you can . . ." This loving and supportive Christ has two hands, one to help us along and the other to point the direction. Never aspire to any goal that would be displeasing to him.

Do not set a goal as an end in itself. This can only lead to depression. Graduation is a worthy goal. It is a significant achievement. The person who sees it as an end in itself is soon to experience a letdown. Goals should be seen as gateways. They are merely portals for passage through to others. Each gateway we go through is a reward, but we come to it only to go through it. With this in mind there is occasion for being happy over an objective reached. Likewise, there is no big letdown over "what next?" This outlook results in steady progress.

Never elbow others aside to reach your goal. If you can reach your objective only by trampling the weaker and slower, it is too great a price to pay. Those who win the truest success are never in such a hurry to reach their goal that they can't hold out a helping hand to those of less strength.

Be patient in striving for your goals. Give yourself time—a lifetime. Expect some resistance. Learn from the bubble. Bubbles rise to the top of water in a spiraling manner—not straight up. The resistance caused by the water causes the spiral. You too can expect obstacles. Accept them as challenges and occasions to prove your desire and demonstrate your determination. Be like the bubble that seems to know it is not going anywhere but up. It is patient in getting there.

Determine your rights. What privileges and opportunities allow you to strive for your purpose? You deserve the best—your best. It is your right and responsibility to strive to be and to accomplish your best. Do not use anyone else as a measuring rod. You are the standard by which you should be measured.

You have the right to fulfill your maximum responsibility. Don't die with your song unsung, your race unrun. Avoid going through life looking for someone to blame. The "you-made-me-do-it" complex drives people away. Accept the fact that you are a free moral agent with the capacity to choose and do. Society doesn't owe you anything. It has provided an environment in which you can strive and struggle just like everybody else. Earn your way. Pay the price.

You have the right to see your needs and try to fulfill them. A mechanic who failed four times in business made an observation. Modern buildings were being constructed taller. People were complaining about climbing stairs. His determination produced a device that made modern skyscrapers possible. Elisa Otis invented the elevator. The Otis Elevator Company is still a major contributor to the industry.

An aspiring preacher had a "hopeless hobby" of toying with rubber. He saw a need and energetically worked to meet it. That young man, Charles Goodyear, discovered a method of vulcanizing rubber, and a whole new industry was born.

The manager of a broom factory, and later a sanitarium, saw the need for a breakfast food. His "fooling around" in the kitchen paid off. Will Kellogg produced a new breakfast cereal.

These persons realized they had a right to work against odds and to produce. This was their right. It is not unlike yours. Your limitations are not unlike theirs.

Develop self-trust. When overwhelmed by a sense of

fault, frailties, and failures, remember that no one is perfect. Confidence does not come from an absence of these things. It results from rebounding from them.

It was said that Frederick the Great of Prussia was once walking along a road on the outskirts of Berlin when he accidentally brushed against an old man.

"Who are you?" the king asked out of idle curiosity as his walk came to an abrupt halt.

"I am a king," answered the old man.

"A king? Over what principality do you reign?" asked the amazed Frederick.

"Over myself. I rule myself because I control myself. I am my own subject to command," replied the elderly man with pride.

If you can't control yourself, you can't trust yourself. Like a maddened animal you might destructively break out and injure someone, as well as yourself. Know what you can trust yourself with. Drugs, alcohol, a sensuous, promiscuous environment, and bad companions are influences that can cause one to lose control of self. Don't even trust yourself around those influences. Avoid them altogether.

Every person has areas where he can't trust self. The diabetic can't trust himself to eat too many sweets. The amputee can't trust himself in a sprint. A warm-blooded human being can't trust himself in a pit with snakes. Identify your weaknesses and areas of self-defeat and avoid them with pride. Control yourself. Be the king of your conscience. Can you trust yourself to protect yourself by discipline to do the proper things? Develop your self-trust.

Dedicate your life. Commit your ways unto the Lord. Nothing is worth doing that is not done "as unto the Lord." If it is worth doing, it is worth asking his blessings on it. If you can't ask his blessings on it, it is not worth doing. Drop it.

Perhaps as a child you tried to pick yourself up by your

shoe strings. There have been some strenuous struggles by persons trying this feat. Try as we may, none have been successful. The downward pull of gravity exceeds any effort we might exert.

Trying to live life without the uplift given by faith in Jesus Christ is just as foolish. The struggle may be genuine, sincere, and courageous. But it always ends the same—unsuccessful, futile.

Dedicate your life to doing what the Lord in the Bible has asked of you. He has never once asked you to do anything that is not for your good. He has never suggested that you not do anything for any reason other than it is best for you not to do. Every request God makes is, from the divine perspective, perfectly logical. All are for our good.

Naaman was a Bible character with the dread disease of leprosy. The Lord told him to bathe in the waters of the Jordan River. He did and was healed. There was no healing quality about the water of the river.

The children of Israel were told to place a brass serpent on a pole and look at it for healing of their snakebites. They did and were healed. There was no healing quality in brass to cure a snakebite.

In each instance it was faithful obedience to God's word that accomplished the healing. The people were dedicated to him. They had to walk by faith, not by sight. They could not see how doing these things could accomplish the intended end. They did it out of dedication and obedience.

Compliance with the Word of God always results in that which is best for the doer.

A simple Scriptural statement serves to illustrate this. Often we are confronted with situations where the only way out seems to be: do something we know is in itself wrong. But by doing it the pressure of a given situation can be eased or a problem seemingly solved. Is it right to do one wrong to correct another?

Careful now! What if the second wrong seems little compared to the first? Suppose doing the second will take the heat off you and put it on someone else. It could be exhausting to have to make this decision every time there is such a situation. Therefore, in love, the Lord has already given us the answer. It is simply, "Don't do evil that good may come."

When one is dedicated to doing God's will, decision-making is simplified. It then becomes just a matter of doing what is defined. Remember the definition is made with your welfare in mind. It is always for your good. This is true because it is made by a God who is always a good God.

Dedication to the Lord has changed many lives. *Abraham* lied to the Lord. After dedicating his life to the Lord he became a faithful and true servant of the Lord. *Jacob* was a swindler. Repentantly, he dedicated his life to the Lord and became known as "a prince with God." *Jonah* ran from God. His dedication resulted in his becoming an instrument of power and grace.

Moses was a murderer. At the burning bush scene on Mt. Sinai, he dedicated his life to the Lord. Thereafter, his life was a display of the power of God. *David* committed adultery. As a renewed servant of the Lord, he became known as "a man after God's own heart." *Simon Peter* denied his Lord. Later he became God's tool to preach on the occasion of Pentecost when 3,000 persons gave their lives to Christ. In each instance, dedication to the living Lord changes lives. It is an ingredient needed in every life.

The dedicated life is the confident life. Christ commented, "Without me ye can do nothing" (John 15:5). An additive shows the potential of you and Christ together,

"With God all things are possible" (Matt. 19:26).

In light of this, the person whose life is dedicated to serving the Lord can approach any situation and know that if a job is to be done, it can be done because of God's support.

Truly dedicated people plan to give themselves for a cause without reservation. The giving is the cause for satisfaction, not the outcome. A successful outcome is merely a second victory. The primary victory is won in the moment of dedication.

When the Romans first laid siege to Britain, they were defeated. The lapse of time brought their boats once more to the horizon off the shores of Dover. The Anglo-Saxons watched from the cliffs as the Romans came ashore. Carefully, the Romans unloaded their supplies and men. Then they pushed their ships out to sea after setting a torch to them. The defenders looked on in fright, knowing the Romans had come to conquer or give their lives in the attempt. Such fierce dedication that left no means of retreat unnerved the defenders. Rome conquered.

As you build your courage by dedicating your life to the Lord, plan no retreat. Burn your boats. Give yourself confidently.

In no way can a person really guarantee his future. The best that can be done is to size up the opportunities, evaluate the risks, estimate his ability to deal positively with those risks, and then make plans—with confidence.

This proves trust in the Lord.

4. What Makes Your Boat Float

Jesus Christ has promised to meet our needs. These are times when it seems he will have to be very busy to keep that promise. As you walk through the uplands of victory, achievement, and success, he will be with you to meet your needs. This is evident. When you walk through the valley of the shadow of death, he will also be with you. This is not always so evident. Yet, it is no less a fact.

The quality of life God has promised those who follow him is spoken of as "abundant life." This means life with super additives. It involves giving life a purpose, meaning, direction, and guidance. This reveals him to be a loving heavenly Father with exceptional ability and love. He wants to be your support.

Three aspects of his support deserve your attention.

As a former Louisiana resident, I enjoyed deep-sea fishing far out in the Gulf of Mexico. This often took us out of sight of land. One fishing companion owned a number of oil rigs in the Gulf. These large, warehouse-like structures were built above the water. Occasionally we would board a rig for lunch.

This part of the Gulf had just been raked by hurricane-force winds of over 150 M.P.H. All personnel abandoned the rigs during such storms.

One day as I walked around the deck, I happened to look over the side. Beneath the platform were three massive support columns. They pierced the clear water's surface and stretched deep to the Gulf's floor. There they rested on large concrete foundations. Reaching down into the belly of the earth were large shafts. Through them was pumped "black gold" called oil. When the storms struck, these platforms remained stable. They were secure because of the three support columns. Consider each of them illustrative of God's supports for your life.

Reflect on the life of Abraham. His experience clearly depicts three supports now available to you. Abraham's life is a miniature of many. His story illustrates principles also included in the New Testament.

God expressed his will for Abraham. The Lord called on him to do a specific thing. One of the most stabilizing influences in your life should be your—

Calling

If you know Christ personally as your Savior, there is only one reason. God the Father called you by his Holy Spirit to trust God the Son, Jesus Christ. This is a universal calling which he extends in love. Many reject it. Others receive it and revel in it.

The Father does not quit calling at that point. He continues to direct his children. This guidance is often referred to as "his calling." Some people like to think that God calls certain people to do special things because those people are exceptional. Various individuals brag on persons who know and are doing God's will. Many feel that those called must have some unusual ability, a unique vitality, or extraordinary dynamic. People seem to think God looks down and says, "That is such a wonderful person, I am going to use him."

Occasionally someone will apply this attitude toward himself. They are like the Harvard freshman who arrived on campus in time to celebrate the university's 300th birthday.

He exlaimed, "It took Harvard 300 years to get ready for me."

God never has called anyone because of one's virtue or vitality. The calling of Abraham helps to reveal this truth. When called, Abraham was a member of an idol-worshiping family in an area called Ur. His ancestors worshiped idols. He did also. The Scripture reveals that three generations of his family were still worshiping idols after Abraham left the country.

Abraham was not called simply because he was so good God couldn't do without him.

The great faith of Abraham was not the reason for his calling. At the time of his calling, he had no faith at all. God called him, and then as the Scripture said, "Abraham believed God." God did not call him because he had great faith but that he might manifest faith.

God's calling, his leadership, is still available for every person. It is never granted because of merit on our part. There was a reason expressed for God's call of Abraham. It is the only explanation for his guidance. Stated simply the reason for God's giving divine guidance is: "I love you." That is the only reason anyone is ever given supernatural assistance. It is reason enough. It is God's nature to guide. It is his job. Let him.

Be sure you are where you are and are doing what you are doing because it is God's will. Then, when the storms of life come you can know you are where you are because God loves you. When things are rocky, reflect on the truth—you are loved with a heavenly love. When problems and pains come, remember you are an object of divine love.

Faith is merely believing God and trusting him. That is exactly what Abraham did. He believed God.

Some people profess they cannot live by faith. They boast of having a realistic approach to life. "I can't have faith. I would love to, but I just can't," assert some. That is a senseless statement.

Every time you fly in a plane or drive in the rain, faith is being shown. When you buy or sell on credit, faith is being expressed. When you go on a date or take a mate, you are demonstrating great faith. It is a natural, everyday part of life.

Your linkage with Christ does not leave you without responsibility. He works in the believer as the believer works for him. "*We* can do it," is a good motto for life. A further definition of "we" is appropriate. "The Lord + you and me = we." This was the spirit of the apostle Paul who said, "I can do all things through Christ which strengtheneth me" (Phil. 4:13).

> The Lord and I grew a bed of flowers
> He really did the most
> but it was ours.
>
> We used
> His fresh air,
> His warm sun,
> His pure water,
> His rich soil,
> His life principle.
>
> My part was so unimportant that I said,
> "Lord, you grow this flower bed.
> Of me you have no need
> You grow the seed.
> Lord, you can do it alone,
> I'll rejoice when everything is grown."
>
> "Never," He said, "this is our flower bed.
> I'll do my part, but I'm waiting for you to start.

You pull the weeds
 I'll germinate the seeds."

So I did my feeble best
 He did all the rest.
God gave life to the little seed,
 Showered it with all the rain it might need,
Drew it with sunshine hour after hour
 Until we had a beautiful flower.
Next He turned to me and said,
 "Your life is like that flower bed.
 If you will work with me
 We'll make it a thing of beauty to see."

"I'll provide," He said—
 "The showers of blessings.
 There will be help from above
 The sunshine of love.

"Count on me to set the seed free.
 My grace will be the soil
 But you have got to toil.
You do the digging," said He,
 "And I don't want any reneging."

Then said I, "Lord, make me after thy will,
 My cup I want you to fill.

"Do your work, I can't, but
 You just make me a saint.
Give me great faith, humble me
 Make me a giant just for thee.
With compassion I want to be filled.
 By me I want others to be thrilled."

"Okay," He said, "But
>You have to till your heart
Clear it of evil, that's your part.
>>Let grow only your very best.
>>>Get rid of all the rest
You follow, fish, grow, and go
>Let's see how well you can hoe.
I will cultivate you as—
>Productive
>Beautiful
>Fruitful
>Useful
>Anything
But only if you do your part.
>This is only the beginning" . . .
>>>>START.

Faith is the ingredient that puts you in business with the Lord. He calls—you answer. Faith is not belief in spite of proof. It is trust in spite of consequence. Faith sees the invisible, believes the incredible, and receives the unimaginable.

There may be many things in life you don't understand. Many questions without apparent answers may arise. Doubt may attempt to block your path. In these and other crises, just remember—a loving God cares for you. Keep your faith in the fact that there is an answer, an explanation, and a solution. Keep that faith alive.

We trust people. We believe strangers when they give us directions to unknown destinations. We rely on unknown instructors who advise us on everything from math to manners. We trust doctors we have never before seen when they prescribe. We accept the counsel of lawyers we know only by reputation. "If we receive the witness of men, the witness of God is greater" (1 John 5:9).

Some persons never venture to do what they know to be right in God's sight. They fail to try because they fear they will falter. You might falter. Actually, you likely will, sometimes. To refuse to try, though, because you might fail is certainly to fail. Abraham faltered. He was called by God to go from Ur to Canaan. He stopped for several years in a place called Haran. God did not discard him. In love God called him again. That time Abraham responded and God guided. Do not desire to or design a falter. Neither be defeated by it. Response and realignment after every stumble can actually move you closer to an intended goal.

A second strategic support in life is . . .

Character

The character of God is a reliable resource. His character and power to perform are illustrated in the story of Abraham's pilgrimage.

Four powerful kings had invaded the Land of Promise which Abraham was to inherit. These four swept across the land like locusts. They laid waste the territory of their conquest. Cities were pillaged. They looted the land. As was the custom, to the victor went the spoils of war. The wealth of the people was stripped away from them.

In their conquest of the land, they bypassed Abraham. His holdings were so small and his power so puny they simply ignored him and his limited resources.

Abraham was at the mercy of the kings. He was defenseless. To him the Lord said, "I am thy shield" (Gen. 15:1). That is a beautiful revelation of the character of God. He does not abandon his people, regardless of overwhelming odds.

It is not too unrealistic to compare those kings to forces that will conquer any person who does not have God as a shield.

Bitterness is one emotion that will conquer a heart un-shielded by the Lord. Bitterness stains all thought. It colors every attitude. Bitterness and its young brother, resentment, produce an unhealthy outlook on life. Many become bitter because others have more than they. Some show bitterness because of a lack of success. Failure to be recognized in a hoped-for way can cause bitterness. Jealousy is a mark of bitterness and jealousy reveals more self-love than love.

Resolve never to be bitter. It will serve only to warp your personality. Don't let it divert you from your goal. Never let it keep you from venturing down new paths of endeavor. It should never cause you to be so insistent of your rights that you fail to discharge faithfully your obliga-tions and responsibilities.

Ask the Lord to shield you from the devastating attacks of bitterness.

A second common king is *temptation.* Temptation is any attraction to do or think or say wrong in God's sight. The Scriptures give guidelines regarding right and wrong. People who are persuaded to smell the "sweet" blossoms of temptation must be prepared to eat its bitter fruit. Resisting temptation builds character.

The person who is suddenly overpowered by tempta-tion has usually been dreaming about something for a long time. Run from temptation and don't leave a forwarding address. When you face it, turn to the right. If it knocks at your door, ask Christ to answer the knock for you.

Build your moral muscle by resisting the ever-recurring small temptations. This will help you to be strong when the big ones come.

It is like the myth about the youth who picked up the newborn calf in the field. Every day he returned and picked it up in his arms. The calf's weight increased only slightly each day. Such a small increase was not noticeable. As he lifted the calf daily, the boy's strength grew with the calf's weight. This continued until the growing lad could lift the grown, full-sized bull.

Temptations are common. Every person has them. Be glad that the Lord will provide a way to escape them (1 Cor. 10:13). Temptation is a disguised appeal to keep you from the best things for you. Any appeal to do evil is a booby trap.

Ask the Lord to shield you from the disillusioning attacks of temptation.

A third tyrant king in many lives is *guilt*. Forgiveness is the shield against it. Nothing else is sufficient. Rationalization, compromise, comparisons, and a blasé attitude will not last long as a defense.

He who confesses his guilt avoids a trial. The verdict of one's own heart has never acquitted any person. Guilt cannot keep its own secret. Repentance is the only successful solution. Forgiveness, divine forgiveness, is the single remedy and release.

Often persons are known to say, "I can't forgive myself." This is an acknowledgment that guilt is ever-present with the person. Such a statement is in fact true. No one can forgive self. The Lord has never given this authority to any person. It is still the exclusive right of God. So persons must seek God's forgiveness. After doing so, do not go away remorseful of guilt, but rejoicing over grace. If you ask for God's forgiveness, accept the fact that you are forgiven. The cause for guilt is cured. Thank God.

Ask the Lord to shield you from the depleting attacks of guilt.

The fourth and commanding king is *Satan*. There is a renewed awareness of his influence in our society. A devil consciousness has alerted people to the fact of his existence. His supernatural power is greater than our ability to resist it.

49

But great comfort belongs to the believer in that, "Greater is he that is in you (Christ), than he that is in the world (the devil)" (1 John 4:4).

Four literal kings confronted Abraham. His responsibility was to counterattack. He did so with an awareness that the Lord was his shield. The results were miraculous. He defeated the four kings and recovered the spoils of their conquest. His shield had prevailed.

The third basic support in life is . . .

Capacity

The capacity of the Lord, not the individual, is what gives assurance and stability. The character of God was revealed in his promise: "I am . . . thy great reward (Gen. 15:1).

After his victory, Abraham gave Melchizedek one-tenth of the wealth he had obtained from the kings. This tithe was payed to Melchizedek as acknowledgment that God had provided everything. This is still a good practice. Abraham next went to the king of Sodom and gave him all the remaining bounty. So, Abraham had nothing left. This was most uncommon for a conqueror like Abraham. He had no reward for his work. At this point the Lord promised to be Abraham's reward.

The reward Abraham would receive was indicated in the names by which he knew God. Each of these Hebrew names is translated "God" in the Bible.

He knew him as *Jehovah*. This name means "I am," hence, the eternally existing one.

He knew him as *Jehovah-Jireh*. This name means "the God who provides."

He knew him as *El Elyon*. This name means "the Most High God."

So Abraham knew God as the eternally existing God

who provides—the Most High God. It is this One who promised to be his reward.

This same God makes this same provision for you. All believers are spoken of as being "... heirs of God, and joint-heirs with Christ" (Rom. 8:17). In this way an inheritance is promised the child of God, a reward.

If there is more than one heir to a piece of property, each owns only a portion. For example, if five heirs inherit five acres, each one receives one acre. Joint heirs are different. If five joint heirs inherit five acres, each owns all five acres equally with the other four. Each owns the total—everything. Joint heirs mutually possess *all*, together.

The believer is a joint heir with Jesus Christ. All that is his is yours. When Abraham gave himself and his resources to the Lord, he found the Lord had already given Himself and His resources to him. This is still true.

An experience from my youth illustrates this vital principle.

Our Sunday School class was going on a picnic. Each person was to prepare his own lunch. This had to be done without any help. My speciality was banana/peanut butter sandwiches. I mashed up a couple of bananas and mixed them with peanut butter. In a short time my sandwiches were ready.

We gathered at the church. The walk to the wooded picnic area was short. However, there was one pretty young friend I felt obligated to help. She was always sweet and kind. Besides, her dad was rich. I offered to carry her picnic basket. She said, "That is a good idea." With my pail in hand and her basket on arm we set off on our picnic.

I had heard her talking about the contents of her basket. She had a fried chicken, six homemade blueberry muffins, potato salad, stuffed eggs, several slices of cake, and a half-gallon jug of iced tea. She also had one of her mother's best tablecloths, napkins, and silverware. I took good care of her and her picnic basket.

When lunchtime came she said, "Why don't we spread our lunches together?" I said, "That is a very good idea." We did.

We sat down and opened her lunch basket and my lunch pail and spread all we had together. All she had was mine and all I had was hers. We shared equally.

Spiritually, that is true. The moment that all you have is Christ's, all that Christ has is yours. You share jointly.

It would have been foolish if I had refused to share my meager lunch with one who was willing to share a feast with me. So it is unwise if I refuse to give all that I have to One who has given all that God has to me.

The capacity of the eternally existing God who provides, the Most High God, is at your disposal. His resources become yours the moment yours become his.

5. Sweet Sorrow

One of the most anxious moments in your parents' lives come when you first started down a flight of stairs without their holding your hand. If a film of the experience existed it would probably reveal your parents reaching out, though not quite touching you.

The parents were accustomed to holding your hand. You were used to them doing it. Now on the stairs a parting happened. They let go and you toddled on—one unsure, the other uncomfortable. The parent was relinquishing a role. You were assuming a new one. It was an awkward moment.

As in that experience, so now in a time of graduation, a similar emotion exists in a growing relationship. The parent is always reluctant to let the hand go. Because of love for the infant, parents want to protect and provide. Parents are uncertain because they have seen other children fall.

The fact that you had never before walked down steps by yourself made them all the more fearful. But, as reluctant as they might have been, they eventually let go of your hand. No matter how many times you fell, you finally made it down the stairs.

In most instances, the child is unaware of the parents' concern. A sense of independent confidence drives the shaky toddler on. As this confidence grows, adventures are undertaken. As more success is enjoyed, the parents let go more and enjoy watching their developing child.

Graduation time is a grown-up moment equivalent to the stair experience. For the first time, now a new independence is being established. Again the child is seldom as concerned as the parent. The parents are concerned having fallen themselves and having seen many young people fall in young adulthood. Even the most confident and trusting parents are. This prompts some parents to want to hold on. Inevitably this cannot continue. Sooner or later they must let go.

Holding on has given the parents a sense of worth and value. Now your emergence robs them of a job they have enjoyed. A fulfilling role in their lives has lessened. This often leaves parents feeling a little empty. They are no longer needed as before.

This sounds sad, but it is natural and essential. A parent must realize this is healthy and proper. A child must recognize this is painful for both parties. Timing is crucial. If a parent lets go too soon, the immature offspring fails. If they hold on too long, the ambitious youth rebels. Liberty must be earned and given. When given, it must be the occasion to prove one's worth and gain more.

Parting is still sweet sorrow.

In all of life, it is instinctive for a person to gather to oneself the object of love and to protect it. A little child enjoys protecting a pet or doll. There is a clinging aspect of love. Developing friendships involves this same emotional relationship. There is a desire to be with and share together with the object of our love.

Courtship is a time when this feeling reaches a new high. In marriage it is a basic ingredient. It is true in all of life—with one exception, parenthood. In parenthood one rears the object of love to give it away. This is contrary to all other relationships. So, it is a strange and strained experience.

Graduation is a new separation. It is a parting of parent and child. The child must go. The parent must let go.

Any child leaving home must take this into account. Though a new independence has been earned and gained, a debt of gratitude remains. A geographical distance may develop, but an emotional closeness emerges. A young adult leaving home should remember that the parents have just done the unnatural thing of giving up an object of their love. Make sure to write home. Phone home. Go home. The frequency of such contacts decreases, but the freshness can increase. Don't let your parents down—they brought you up.

In the quest for independence, don't injure your parents. If they want to give you something—anything—with no strings attached, and you can use it, accept it and enjoy it. If there are no strings attached, there is no obligation. By accepting parental gifts the child is letting the parent express a still strong love. By refusing to accept a nonobligatory gift, simply because of obstinate independence, one crushes loving grace. A gift can help both the recipient and the giver. Let such help happen, if at all possible.

Now is a grand time to pay back your parents in a refreshing way. Make a note of their birthdays, anniversaries, and other important events in their lives. Send a card or contact them on these special days. The cost is minimal, but the investment of love pays big dividends. It will be gratifying to the grateful parent and satisfying to the thoughtful you. Don't take time to do this; *make* time to do it. Mark these events on a calendar as a reminder to your well-intending, forgetful self.

Our lives emerge from a "me"-centered world to a "you"-oriented one. In infancy, wants and needs are asserted without regard for the welfare of others. It might have been late at night when you awakened your parents because you wanted your bottle. There might have been a party going on when you demanded what you wanted at some very unusual times. As you grew older you demanded a drink of water by pulling on your parent's arm and interrupting a conversation with a whiny cry. You had to have what you wanted when you wanted it. Gradually you have put more of your own wants and wishes aside in consideration of what will benefit others.

A person is only ready for marriage when he has grown from a "me" to a "you" orientation. A grand place to start enlarging your sphere of consideration is with your parents. Perhaps you have always done this. Chances are you might have thought you have, but in reality you haven't. Now is a good time to expand the number of persons you want to please. At this time of separation, you have an opportunity to show great concern for and interest in others by remembering your parents. Even if they have failed you miserably, don't make yourself miserable by failing them. Any deficiency on their part should serve to motivate you not to respond and react as they.

People, miserable people, often live in their own little "me-tight world." Some do not move out easily. Anyone who wants to mature personally and build relationships with others must move out into "their world." When this is done you often find that others have interesting worlds. As you try to move out into the world of your parents, you will find it different but interesting. It too is filled with drama, dreams, dreads, doubts, desires, and delights.

Parent-child separation should occur with courtesy. Two pieces of metal rubbing together can become abrasive and eventually wear each other out. However, if the same two pieces of metal are well-oiled, often they can work together for years without friction. In life experiences, courtesy is that oil. Without it any of life's contacts can cause arguments, disappointments, heartaches, and basic unhappiness. Likewise, persons can work together for years without conflict and confrontation. What makes the difference? Courtesy.

A wise sage once said, "Life is not so short but that there is always time enough for courtesy."

Basic good manners and common courtesy should be shown in establishing and relinquishing relationships. Practice on your parents.

"With patience a ruler may be persuaded, and a soft tongue will break a bone" (Prov. 25:15, RSV).

Everyone has moods. Big events dramatically affect moods. Graduation is a big event. Graduation influences one's moods. It is a big event for the graduate and for friends and family. Understanding must be exercised. It is a superb time to interpret each other on the basis of the love that is known, rather than on what is said and done. Work to assert your mind over your mood. The reverse can produce problems.

Parting is made easier if accompanied by *compliments*. Most graduates have an elevated self-image. This is understandable. Graduation is an achievement worthy of a sense of fulfillment. Many people lavish praise on graduates. Obtaining a job or going off to college is also commendable. Again, compliments come to the achiever. This is a constructive time when self-worth is at a new high.

Meanwhile, the parent may be suffering from a sagging self-concept. Life becomes more meaningful when we feel accepted. Compliments can reassure a person. Do not bypass people who have made a vital contribution to your life. Friends, teachers, and most of all parents are worthy of your compliments.

Insecure persons find it difficult to compliment others. Those who enjoy good emotional and mental health find it comparatively *easy* to compliment others. It is gratifying for them to properly praise others.

In telling your friends good-bye, do not hesitate to tell them how much they have meant to you. It is emotional but ultimately will be a refreshing memory. Make it a point to say "thanks" to your folks also. Your new status gives you cause to feel comfortable in complimenting them.

In a time of separation, persons are more comfortable when there is *cooperation.* Share your plans. You might be amazed how reassured your parents would be by knowing your ambitions and aspirations. Plans can and well might change. Yet, some tension is removed if there is a common insight about your desires and drives.

Do not hesitate to ask their advice. Let them know where you want to go—and why—and how you expect to achieve your goals—and when. Give them a chance to boost and support you. Few graduates feel a need for such, but don't forget, the parents do. If the help of the parents is needed financially or any other way, let them know from the beginning. Give them a chance to share in the biggest adventure of one they love. Even if you cannot agree on every aspect, do attempt to be cooperative.

Separation from the comforts of home, departure from the familiar, and removal from a friendly environment also has a dramatic impact on the graduate. Anytime we confront the unknown or unfamiliar, there is a degree of uncertainty and fear.

In growing certain types of plants it is necessary to separate small plants growing from the roots of the parent plant, so the younger ones might grow and develop. Properly transplanted young plants can often grow to maturity more rapidly. The parent plant also is allowed to continue producing. Eventually a child must cut free and become an independent individual.

Some children feel a bit of guilt in doing so. They love their parents and feel an obligation to them. Both facts are true. It is good to love them, and it is proper to realize an obligation to them. The obligation, however, is not necessarily to stay with them but to develop to your full potential. Love for them prompts a child to make such a mature move.

If one compromises and sacrifices integrity, the gold of his being remains unmined, his gifts undeveloped, and his abilities decay. One major drive in every life should be self-actualization. Nothing satisfies the need for growth but growth. An objective in life is to grow and to keep on growing as long as life lasts. The alternative is not good. It is spoken of in a French proverb: "Qui ne s'avance pas recule," that is, "Whoever does not go forward goes backward."

Hang this couplet on the pegboard of your mind.

"If you think you're green, you'll grow;
If you think you're ripe, you'll rot."

"Happiness," observed Aristotle, "is the fulfillment of function. And no man is happy except in proportion as he fulfills his function in life." Make one of your goals to move toward wholeness in life. Find your function and fulfill it. You will find, as a result, parents who feel fulfilled.

One form of separation is rebellion. No youth has ever been willing to accept the world as he found it. Every generation wants to change it. That is good. Such an attitude has produced much of our progress. Pasteur, Emerson, Salk, Marconi, Webster, Lincoln, and Glenn were not willing to accept the world as they found it. They wanted to change it. They changed it by improving it. No child must aspire to be like his parent. Every child *should* desire to be better in the sense of more completely fulfilling his function in life.

Any vent of a rebellious nature should be against injustice, unfairness, laziness, immorality, and greed. If you are intent on destroying and replacing something, make sure it is replaced with something of more benefit to more people. And be certain it is acceptable to the Lord.

In an impatient rush to independence, do not ruin your relations with others. A Cajun proverb speaks to the wisdom of not upsetting relationships: "Never insult the alligator until you have crossed the bayou." So, never knock the achievements of others until you have accomplished your ultimate. Then there will be little time or desire to put down anyone.

In parting, be sure you—

"Honour thy father and thy mother . . ." (Ex. 20:12).

Be sure the home you walk away from is the home you can come back to.

6. Pick A Mountain

Has it every happened to you? There is homework to be done. You have just settled in. No sooner have you gotten started than someone phones to ask about another assignment. Your promise to look it up and call them back.

As you start to your other books, you notice the mail has come. You have to glance at it. It will take only a minute. The letter on top contains a comment about a friend next door. That reminds you of something you want to share. It will take only a minute to run next door. On the way through the kitchen you are seized by a sudden hunger attack. You decide to interrupt your busy schedule for a quick snack. Your accomplishments so far—exactly nothing.

It is easy to stay busy and do nothing. The only way to avoid it is to plan your activities. Take a bit of time and list the things you must do in order. Do not let anything, short of another world war, interrupt you. If you are interrupted, immediately go back to the last unfinished job. Do not leave a job half done and start another.

Stick-to-it-ness is a quality that makes for productivity. President Calvin Coolidge wisely encouraged it: "Nothing in this world can take the place of persistence. Talent will not; nothing is more common than unsuccessful men with talent. Genius will not; unrewarded genius is almost a proverb. Education will not; the world is full of educated derelicts. Persistence and determination alone are omnipotent. The

61

slogan 'press on' has solved and always will solve the problems of the human race."

Be a finisher. Never quit. Don't allow yourself the luxury of being distracted. Stay with a project until it is finished.

"Whatsoever ye do, do it heartily, as to the Lord, and not unto men" (Col. 3:23).

Anything worth doing is worth doing well. Put your heart into every assignment. The full thrust of your being can move the immovable. In contact sports, an athlete can be badly injured by trying to hold back. In any event of life, great loss can be sustained by not going all out. Never tolerate yourself the excuse, "I could have done it if I had wanted to."

Choose a Supervisor to inspect your work. Do what you do "as to the Lord." Seek his approval for what you do and the way you do it. Don't be a manpleaser.

Seek the Lord's approval for all that you do. If you work heartily in a manner pleasing to him, you have accomplished the ultimate.

Then if persons disapprove, there is no cause for despondency. You know you did your best, and you did it for the Lord's approval. The fact that others disapprove does not defeat you.

If you perform your duty "as to the Lord" and people applaud the result, there is room for an ego trip. It was not their approval you sought, but his. Their approval is gratifying, but his is satisfying.

This attitude keeps you striving for your best. It also takes off the pressure of criticism. You can rest when you know you have done your best.

Find something worth doing and do it. There will be many to tell you why it can't be done. There will seldom be those who will help you do it. But, if your chosen task is worth your time, it is worth your best effort.

The late Walt Disney built a motion-picture empire. He was an innovator. In part he explained his success. When he came up with what he thought was a fresh, new idea, he would call his three most trusted co-workers together. If, after he explained it to them, they said it couldn't be done, he set out to do it. The fact that something hasn't been done by us or we've never seen it done, doesn't mean it can't be done.

Sam Jones, preacher of a bygone day, said:

> The longer I live, the more I am certain that the great difference between men—between the feeble and the powerful, the great and the insignificant—is energy, invincible determination—a purpose once fixed, and then death or victory. That quality will do anything that can be done in this world, and no talents, no circumstances, no opportunities, will make a two-legged creature a man without it. There are hindrances without and within, but the outer hindrances could effect nothing if there were no inner surrender to them. Fear of opinion, timidity, dread of change, love of ease, indolence, unfaithfulness, are the great hindrances. Optimism is believing that you can eat the rooster that scratches over your grave.

That is a simple theme we have heard expressed many ways. Maybe it's time we believed it. What is the source of such a positive frame of mind? When traced back to its origin, it is faith in Christ. There is power in Christian faith. That is one reason persons keep going back to the Bible and visiting churches. First John 5:4 is a summary: "This is the victory that overcometh the world, even our faith."

Faith has two facets. It is:

Belief in a fact and Trust of a person.

Imagine that you have all the symptoms of appendicitis. Your side aches. You are suffering from nausea. Fever is another sign of your sickness. Now suppose someone says, "I know just what you need. I have a friend, Dr. Albert Smith. He graduated from the Tulane University School of Medicine. He was number one in his class. He lives at 1234 Beaumont Drive in Marietta, Georgia, with his wife, Trudy, and daughters, Lynn and Sharon. As a practicing surgeon he is considered by his peers as the best in the nation. His phone number is 427-3143. "Do you believe me?"

"Yes!"

"Do you really mean it? You believe me sincerely? Without any reservations?"

"Well, yes, I really believe you."

"Marvelous! You believe. You are cured. You have been healed. You no longer have appendicitis. You can go back to work now."

No. You are not yet well. You have done a marvelous thing. You have believed a fact. That is commendable, but not curative.

To be completely healed you must trust the person. You must trust Dr. Smith enough to let him perform surgery. The moment you yield to his skilled scalpel you are really trusting him. With his medical skills he can remove the cause of your problem and allow the body to recover. You will have demonstrated that you have faith once you couple trust of the proper person with your belief in a fact.

Faith in Christ involves:

> Belief in a fact—He is the Son of God—God the Son.
>> He, the sinless One, died for us, the sinful ones.
>> He is the way, the truth, and the life.

He desires to forgive you and
empower you.

Trust of a person— To trust is to have confidence
in.
It means to "bet your life" on
God.
It involves depending on God
and obeying him.

Once this is done you have a supernatural means of support. Christ said, "Without me ye can do nothing" (John 15:5). Paul said, "I can do all things through Christ" (Phil. 4:13).

All that the Father was to the Son—
the Son wants to be to you.
Once you trust the Son
as the Son trusted the Father
then
He becomes to you what the Father was to him.

When this occurs, the believer has an internal, eternal supply of extraordinary strength. When matched with his intended task for you, it does not matter how difficult the task, for—"Greater is he that is in you than he that is in the world" (1 John 4:4).

To confront the challenges of life, rejoice "For in him we live, and move, and have our being" (Acts 17:28). An awareness of this enables us to rely on him.

Some years ago I had the delight of going on board a submarine in the port of New Orleans. The commanding officer was a friend. He had arranged for me to be on board when they went for a brief underwater cruise. Strange sounds surrounded me as we began to dive. It was a unique sensation realizing our depth as the gauges indicated our descent. Then quietly, almost motionlessly, we reached our cruising depth.

In that moment I was totally dependent on that vessel. The pressure at that depth would have crushed me. Without the vessel I could not have breathed. Yet in it men walked about and did their work. We were—at that moment—living, moving, and having our being, physically, in that submarine. It was our only means of support. It soon became comfortable.

Spiritually, the believer is "in Christ" in a similar way. We are no less dependent on him for our being than the crew of a submarine is dependent on the ship for their existence. The better you know him and the more conscious you are of it, the more comfortable you become. It is a state of security and stability.

As the sub met the challenges of the sea, so Christ meets every challenge confronting us. "The Lord is good, a stronghold in the day of trouble; and he knoweth them that trust in him" (Nah. 1:17). Rejoice!

Three great challenges are worth noting.

1. *Insecurity.* Knowing our personal limits, we feel everyone else knows. We develop a complex as though we had signs around our necks listing our liabilities. Strange as it may seem, no one is as aware of your limitations as you. Even more startling is the fact: no one cares half as much as you. By being preoccupied with your liabilities, you put greater limits on yourself. These limits are then projected on difficult tasks, relationships, and ultimately, God. The latter insures a low attainment level. Break the bonds of your limitations. Remember: "For God hath not given us the spirit of fear; but of power, and of love, and of a sound mind" (2 Tim. 1:7).

You are secure in Christ.

2. *Competition.* Expect competition. Let it stimulate

you to excellence. Don't let your competition set your standards, however. Be the real you. Don't be a blurred, cheap carbon copy of everyone else. Show your own distinctives.

A small boy asked a wealthy contractor, who stood watching his latest skyscraper go up, "Sir, how can I be successful like you when I grow up?"

The aging developer spoke kindly. "It is easy, son. Buy a red shirt and work like crazy."

Sensing the lad did not understand, the contractor pointed to the steel structure. "See all those fellows up there? See the one in the red shirt? I don't even know his name. But I've sure noticed how hard he works. His enthusiasm and red shirt stand out. One of these days I'm going to need a new superintendent. When I do I will go up to that fellow and say, 'Hey, you in the red shirt, come here!' He'll get his big chance!"

Stand out. To overcome the competition, stand out. Even if it means wearing a red shirt. But don't plan to make it by being all shirt and no sweat.

3. *Disapproval.* No one likes disapproval. Everyone gets it sooner or later. Most often sooner than later. If you deserve it, learn to live better because of it. If you don't deserve it, learn to love more because of it. Don't let the fear of disapproval freeze you into inactivity. If you dare not venture for fear of disapproval, you have denied your potential. There is always the chance of disapproval. When you get disapproval remember it can be one of the best things ever to happen in your life.

It can correct your errors, adjust you deficiencies, nudge you to better performance. Resolve never to let it defeat you.

Let disapproval make you a better person, not a bitter person.

7. Come Hades or High Water

Jamestown was flooded. The water rose to a depth of six feet. Two friends allegedly sat on a rooftop and watched it flow by. Amid the floating debris was an old hat. It flowed by, stopped, turned around, and came back upstream against the tide. Reaching a certain point, it again reversed itself and started downstream. This process repeated itself several times as they watched in amazement. Finally, one of them said, "I know what it is. Grandpaw said he was going to mow the grass today come hell or high water!"

That's commitment!

Commitment anticipates obstacles and accepts them as part of the price paid for achievement. Adversity is looked on as an opportunity to prove capacity and commitment. Limitations are not liabilities, but occasions to overcome restrictions and assert one's character, even when capacity can't conquer. Dogged determination is another phrase for commitment.

Leonardo da Vinci, considered by many the greatest genius of all time, wrote:

> O Lord,
> Thou givest us everything,
> At the price
> Of an effort.

The apostle Paul wisely observed, "I can do all things through Christ which strengtheneth me" (Phil. 4:13). This text reveals a dynamic partnership. It consists of "I" and "Christ." Human ingenuity and effort reach a new peak of productivity when combined with divine guidance.

Commitment means . . .

Being Captivated by an Obsession

What is your obsession? Everybody has or develops one. Make sure yours is a worthy one.

I watched an old man shuffle along the edge of an interstate highway. His clothes were worn and dirty. Where did he come from? What happened? Is this all there is to life for him? Did it all have to end this way? I passed and never saw him again, but he is there in my mind. Those questions are still to be answered. Or perhaps those are not the right questions. Questions like, "Where am I going? What am I going to make happen? How can I find and enjoy the meaning of life? Does it all have to end like this?"

That man likely had not experienced more defeats, disappointments, and disillusionments than any other person. We all will have difficulties and disasters. They are inevitable. Studies indicate that most people have an average of three major crises in their lifetimes. That many, or more, appear on life's horizon for each of us. Some are bigger than others, but they are there. Our commitment will determine our reaction. Our reaction dictates our direction. The following verse from an anonymous pen speaks to this subject.

If you think you are beaten, you are,
    If you think you dare not, you don't
If you'd like to win, but you think you can't,
    It is almost a cinch you won't.

If you think you'll lose, you're lost,
    For out in the world we find

Success begins with a fellow's will,
    It's all in the state of mind.

If you think you're outclassed, you are,
    You've got to think high to rise,
You've got to be sure of yourself before
    You can ever win a prize.

Life's battle doesn't always go
    To the swifter or faster man,
But sooner or later the man who wins
    Is the man who thinks he can.

An obsession influences all we do. It drives and directs our entire lives. Identify yours. Make sure it is a good one. You will have only one lifetime to fulfill it. It is more important that it relate to what you are than to what you might do. Being is more vital than doing.

It is more important that you be *your best* than to be *the best.* In an athletic contest a superior competitor may defeat all opponents without extending himself. The defeated ones may well have exerted their best efforts. Even their best was not as good as the more gifted person's inferior effort. Yet, the person who does his best and is defeated is not the loser. The winner who did not do his best is the loser. It bears repeating. It is more important that you be *your best* than to be *the best.* Not everyone can win, but everyone can do his best. Be sure that all of life drains you of all your best.

The legendary Coach Vince Lombardi spoke of the joy involved in extending oneself.

"I've never known a man worth his salt who in the long run, deep down in his heart, didn't appreciate the grind, the discipline. . . . I firmly believe that any man's finest hour—is that moment when he has worked his heart out in a good cause and lies exhausted on the field of battle—victorious."

Victorious or not, such a person is never a loser. Only the committed will endure the grind and impose the self-discipline that prompts an exhaustive effort in all of life. Don't spare yourself for the party while there is a game to be won.

Horace Busnell noted, "Life is always dull and insipid to those who have no great works on their hands to do and no lofty ideals to elevate their spirits." A big obsession makes a big person. We tend to take on the size and stature of the goals and responsibilities that consume us.

"The greatest use of time," wrote Williams James, "is to spend it for something that outlasts it." To give one's life in serving the Lord in any life task is gratifying. The pay may be poor, but the retirement benefits are out of this world.

G. K. Chesterton said of Joan of Arc, "She chose her path and went down it like a thunderbolt." She had an obsession and no price was too great to pay for obtaining it—not even her own life. We are each giving out lives for something. Most often it is less dramatically done than by Joan of Arc, but it should never be less decidedly.

Identify your obsession. If you cannot, resolve to establish one. Be patient with yourself in doing it. Always allow yourself the liberty of changing it. Never allow yourself the luxury of lowering your standard simply for the sake of ease. An obsession is something that consumes. Be sure you are the fuel for a worthy fire.

Commitment means . . .

Being Conscious of Obstacles

No path has ever been cleared without first overcoming obstacles. No road has ever been built that didn't require removal of obstacles. These must be dealt with in attempting any worthy objective in life. Expect them. Don't be surprised by them. Never become preoccupied with them. Let them motivate you.

A mountain in your path gives a matchless opportunity to build a tunnel through it, scale its summit, or take the scenic route around it. Never just sit and curse it. Mountains never slink away from the fury of frustration.

Never let an obstacle cause your defeat by responding with one of the following answers.

"I've had it!" Who cares? You will never break the world's heart by quitting. If you have had it, what is the "It" you've had? Does that mean you've paid the maximum price for what you sought? Does it indicate you've used your abilities to their fullest?

"I've had it" often indicates a person is about to quit pursuing a goal and become obsessed with an obstacle. When this happens, the obstacle becomes the goal. At that point you become a negative person.

"I can't!" With that attitude there is no way you can. It is true, "Success comes in cans, not in can'ts." "I can't" means "you ain't." Familiar quotations have a long life because they represent basic truths. One worthy of becoming a plaque on the wall of your mind is, "If at first you don't succeed, try, try again."

"I can't" should be converted to "I haven't been able to—so far." This only indicates the ways you've found in which the job can't be done. That should be encouraging. You are reducing the odds that it can't be done every time you discover another way it can't. You are closer with every failure.

"It won't work." Be sure that's not a disguise for "I won't work at it." Again changing the wording is appropriate, "It hasn't worked—so far." Remember, this is only the beginning. Resolve, "If it is workable, I will find a way to work it." Enjoy a challenge. There is strength in a struggle. There is dignity in doing the difficult.

"It won't work" is often an appeal for someone else to work out your problem. Never be too proud to accept help. Also never be so easily defeated that you call for help too soon. Most things will work if we will work.

"We've never done it that way before." Does that mean that all genius has preceded us? Is it an implication that you have no creativity? Have all the best ideas already been given birth? Change without reason is wrong. Reason for change means there is a new, more practical way at present. To be married to the past is to be divorced from the present.

"We've never done it that way before," suggests an adventure. It implies innovation. This makes many people uncomfortable. The unknown produces uncertainty. Always be open to new, dynamic ways of doing things. Never abandon anything simply because it is familiar. But never let your comfort become an obstacle to new and better ways.

The opportunity for constructive and rewarding achievements in every field is greater than anything we have known, experienced, or dreamed. As long as people can say, "We have never done it that way before," there is a marvelous market for venturesome people.

Albert Einstein stated: "I do not know one hundredth of one percent about anything." If an acknowledged genius like Einstein makes such a confession it indicates there is still much for the present generation to learn and do. This is only the beginning.

Many react like a child that had just learned his multiplication tables all the way to 12 x 12. She was asked, "What is 13 x 13?" She slyly said, "Don't be silly, there is no such thing." Within the realm of her knowledge, there wasn't. In reality, there was. Our multiplication table may end, but multiplication never does. There is much more to follow.

To be a doer you do not have to understand everything. There is motivation in mystery. Enjoy the exciting adventure of learning. Push back the frontiers of your knowledge. Cultivate a thirst for knowledge. Such a pursuit is an exciting adventure. Good books, interesting people, enchanting places, and noteworthy things can aid this quest.

Be aware of obstacles but never be preoccupied with them. An obstacle course is a challenge to athletes. The desire is to overcome, not ignore them. You have the miracle of a human brain with all of its twelve million cells. Do not use it for mundane things. Do not let it be absorbed in what a six-year-old child can do. Use it to run life's obstacle course. It affords a challenge that can be fun—demanding, but fun.

Never confuse obstacles with objections. And don't consider an obstacle to be a valid objection to keep you from starting something worthwhile. There are some valid reasons for not stopping for anything until it stops you:

- If you never start, there is no way you can finish.
- If the difficulty of doing anything retards the starting, then a negative emotion prevails. This makes the task all the more difficult.
- Human judgment makes it difficult to tell an obstacle from an opportunity at a distance. Best and worst often stand close together. Up close it is easy to tell them apart. Many good ideas, even great ones, have been picked to death by cowards. Others have been rendered stillborn by the fear of obstacles that could have been overcome one by one. Don't be afraid of a little opposition. Remember, the "kite" of success rises on the wind of opposition.

> Life by the yard
> is hard.
> By the inch
> it's a cinch.

Every great achievement has been to some extent a bringing of order out of chaos.

Throughout history many creative geniuses and innovators have been very young. The encouraging thing about using your mind creatively is that this capacity improves with age. Start young, and don't let the status quo clog your channels of creativity with the passing of time.

This is only the beginning . . . but don't fail to begin.

Commitment means . . .

Being Challenged to Be Obedient

Let your supreme obedience be to the Supreme Being. Let Christ be Lord of your life. Lord means boss. He deserves to be the one to master your thinking, influence your conduct, and direct your course.

If you are a skeptic having difficulty believing in God, think about this statement by Thomas Edison:

"We don't know the millionth part of one percent about anything. We don't know what water is. We don't know what light is. We don't know what gravitation is. We don't know what enables us to keep our feet when we stand up. We don't know what electricity is. . . . We have lot of hypotheses about these things, but that is all. But we do not let our ignorance about all these things deprive us of their use."

Isn't it reasonable in the 99 + percent of things you do not know, God exists. We must not only believe in God, we must believe him. What he says we should do. At no time in the Bible does he ask us to do anything that is not for our good. At no point does he instruct us to abstain from an action or attitude for any reason than for our good. This is true simply because he loves us. God, who is more knowledgeable and more loving than us, has offered us instructions for living through the Bible.

Do you remember a time that you felt tremendous relief because of the word of a trustworthy friend?

Do you recall being afraid as a child? Then out of the dark came the comforting voice of your parent, "Don't be afraid, I'm here." Has there been a time when your loneliness was dispelled by a friendly voice on the phone speaking words of reassurance?

The word of a competent counselor is often uplifting. There is extraordinary power in words. They can restore confidence, renew intent, revive interest, and reassure persons. The Word of God can do all that. It is the Word of a capable Friend, the voice of a loving Father, and a source of counsel. Be sure you know it. Don't just know *about* it. The Bible contains many promises of power and victory. You need to *know* them.

You will never come in last if you put God first. His Word tells us what to obey and how.

Francis Bacon spoke of it, "There never was found, in any age of the world, either religion or law, that did so highly exalt the public good as the Bible."

Abraham Lincoln noted, "In regards to the Great Book, I have only to say that it is the best gift God has given to man. All the good from the Saviour of the world is communicated to us through this Book."

In Katherine Mansfield's journal she wrote of how she discovered the Bible in her mature years. She had not read it at all while young. At the time of her finding the Scriptures, she was living in a mountain retreat, engaged in a losing fight with tuberculosis. In the tragedy of her sensitive spirit she faced death. Reading the Bible for the first time, she wrote: "I feel so bitterly that I have never known these facts before. They ought to be a part of my very breathing."

Do not wait until your waning years to make them a part of yours. Start now. This is only the beginning.

Immanuel Kant commented, "A single line in the Bible has consoled me more than all the books I ever read besides."

Become acquainted with the Word now so you can apply it to your life. That's how you get wisdom. From wisdom emerges your best self.

King David said, "Thy word have I hid in mine heart, that I might not sin against thee" (Ps. 119:11). Start your own program of hiding today.

The Scripture of letting the Word of God "rule" in your heart. The word translated "rule" is our word for umpire. Let the Word of God call things "safe" and "out" in your life. Let it be the standard for ruling out improper activities. Let it be the umpire to decide right from wrong. Live by its instructions so, ultimately when you reach home (heaven), you will be called "safe."

8. What Storms Your Mind

Once I had a concept that stormed my mind. I conceived of a house of worship that would seat approximately 4,000. The winds of wishing blew often. The water of want nourished it. The sun of desire drew it. After thirteen years of cultivation, the concept became a fact. The idea emerged into a reality.

There are many ideas that dwindle and die. There are never any well-designed facilities, programs, or plans that were not at one time a fleeting thought.

Respect your concepts. Most of your best plans never develop. Many of your best ideas are never given wings. If it is true that you think and envision great things that never happen, why? Who is your worst enemy? You know, the one that frustrates your best concepts? Your parents, teachers, or community leaders? No! If you will be very honest, the one who thwarts most of your best ideas is— YOU.

You do it in a number of ways.

Perhaps you kill many of them by not respecting them. Because an idea is yours does not mean it is either good or bad. It may be either. Some people discount every idea that is theirs because it simply is theirs. They never give it a chance to be tested. It has never occurred to some people that they might have a good idea.

"Success or failure in business is caused more by mental attitude than by mental capacity," said Sir Walter

Scott. Most people have the capacity to succeed, but do not respect it. Never become egotistical. Likewise, never discredit your ideas before they are properly evaluated.

Thoughts rule the world. Your thoughts rule your world. You can make them big enough and good enough to influence others constructively.

"Our life is what our thoughts make it." If the Roman emperor, Marcus Aurelius, spoke truth in that statement, it will be difficult for you to blame others for your failures.

Fear may be the wolf that chokes many of your best concepts to death. Psychologists now list some seven hundred phobias. Apparently, no one is immune from fear. Alphabetically the first phobia is Arachibutyrophobia, the fear of getting peanut butter stuck to the roof of the mouth! There is even a fear of fear, Phobophobia.

From World War II the story emerges of a young soldier's encounter with General Dwight Eisenhower. The youthful combatant told the general of being wounded two weeks earlier. He pleaded not to be sent back into battle. It was the day for an attempt by the Allied Forces to cross the Rhine River. Following many excuses the soldier acknowledged he was afraid. After a period of pleading, the time for action came. General Eisenhower interrupted, "I'm a little afraid also. Let's walk to the river together; it will be good for both of us."

Having walked some distance with the general, the youthful admirer said, "Sir, I *was* afraid . . ."

Even your most-admired hero in truth will concede being a little afraid. Take heart from those who walk by faith. If you have a commendable cause, you also have an Invisible Host. Renew your energy by realizing you do not walk alone.

Never take counsel of your fears.

By lethargy the corpses of many good ideas have been

placed in the grave of "good intentions." Do not let laziness cause you to fail in reaching your potential. Anybody can be lazy. Many excuses are offered for being lazy. None, absolutely none, are acceptable.

There is only a slight difference between a daydreamer and a visionary. A daydreamer awakes and does nothing. The visionary extends himself in helping a concept become a reality.

Daydreamers are numerous and of little value. Visionaries change societies and improve conditions. Action is the additive that makes the difference. There are halls of fame filled with doers. Dreamers die unknown and worst, still unproductive.

Many good ideas are stillborn. Exotic places are supposed to be far away. Exciting events belong to others. Exhilarating ideas are supposed to be conceived by someone else. At least that is the normal way of thinking. Consequently, many people kill their best ideas, never go the required distance, and avoid the exciting adventure. This is true just because they think in this way.

William James capsuled this concept: "Belief creates the actual fact." Achievers achieve because they think they can. They can because they think they can.

Out of Siberia comes this true story which verifies this concept. A Russian railway employee was accidentally locked in a refrigerator car. He knew the type of car he was locked in. As he felt his body growing cold, he scribbled some notes on the wall of the car: "I'm becoming colder." Later, "Still colder." Time lapsed and he continued, "Nothing to do but wait ... I am slowly freezing to death ... Half asleep now, I can hardly write." Finally a faint notation, "These are my last words." They were.

Soon after his lifeless body was found. No physical cause of death could be determined. The boxcar was actually well-ventilated. The temperature in the car was a moderate 56 degrees! The freezing controls had been out of order for some weeks. He was a victim of his own illusions and conclusions. The power of mind over body had won once more.

What is your concept of your capacity? Careful now—in answering that, you are pouring the gelatin of your being into the mold of your self-image. It may last a lifetime once it is set.

> Aspire
> and perspire
> but never retire.

It is important to develop a personal philosophy of life. Every person needs one to help him understand the events of life. Actually everybody has one. Most persons simply have not stopped to think what theirs is.

The apostle Paul stood on Mars Hill in Athens and declared his. The Greek society had many gods. The roadways nearby were lined with statues dedicated to various deities. There was even one dedicated to "the unknown God." It had been erected just in case the citizens had overlooked one. Observing this, Paul spoke of his God.

> "For in him we live,
> and move,
> and have our being"
> (Acts 17:28).

Be absolutely sure your god, as Paul's, is big enough to allow you three liberties.

1. We Exist

There is assurance in knowing you have a God in

which "we live." The living Christ is the one in which a person can *have vitality.*

When a person lives as though the world is God's castle and the territory of his kingdom, there is strength to be gained. The average estimated life span is about a half million hours. Every hour should be lived with the confidence that it is within God's custody.

For a long time I have carried a little card in my wallet to remind me of this fact. It reads:

> The Light of God surrounds me
> The Love of God enfolds me
> The Power of God protects me
> The Presence of God watches over me
> Wherever I am, God is.

In life's storms you can know where you are. In the desert you can know the Person you walk with. In the broad, sunlit beaches you can sense his presence.

In this frame of mind you can know that when difficulties arise, you are matched with God's intended set of problems. They can only serve to challenge and strengthen you. Feel complimented he has trusted you with the situation. He stands ready to help you resolve it. Victory can be yours.

The outstanding Russian author, Tolstoy, told of a time when he sought meaning for his life. He wandered into many hamlets looking for peace and joy. By chance he visited a settlement where the people were happy. The people were so poor that their diet consisted primarily of black bread and water. Tolstoy pleaded, "My friends, you must teach me your secret."

Puzzled by his plea one responded for all, "You, one of the wisest men in Russia, come to us to be taught a secret?"

His insistence resulted in this further response.

"You are created by God. When you stay in contact

with God, then joy is continuous. But if you get away from God, then you get away from the life force. Return to God, my friend; return to His Son, the Saviour, our Lord Jesus Christ, and you will find good days."

We are dependent on the Lord as a spaceperson is dependent on a life-support system. There is little likelihood that any person in outer space would neglect the very system that supports his life. It is constantly monitored, and repeated adjustments are made to maintain that system.

Persons are foolish who try to ignore their spiritual life-support system. As the fish swims in the sea, as the bird flies in the air, so we are dependent on Him for our existence.

When a bucket is dipped into the ocean, the bucket is in the ocean, and the ocean in the bucket. The oceans fills the bucket, but the bucket cannot contain all of the ocean. Likewise, Christ is in the believer, and the believer is in Christ. He can fill us, but he is such a big God we can swim in him.

2. We Exercise

We have a God in which we "move." The living Christ is one in which a person can have *dynamic energy.*

An oil lamp does not give off light. An internal combustion engine does not produce power. It is the oil in the lamp which, when burned, produces light. It is a fuel, such as gasoline, which, when ignited, releases its explosive power. The lamp and engine are designed to utilize the substance that makes them functional. In the Christ/human life equation, Christ is the fuel; the person is the equivalent to the lamp or engine. It is this principle that enables you to " . . . Walk in newness of life" (Rom. 6:4) and "be renewed in the spirit of your mind" (Eph. 4:23).

The physical body is kept active by keeping busy. In addition to normal, daily physical activity it is advisable to engage in a specific exercise program. Such programs are so specific that they can be designed to accomplish intended goals. Some programs are for body building, others for circulatory stimulation, still others for muscle tone. The intended objective determines what exercise is performed.

The spiritual life also requires exercises and drills to keep it alert and vigorous. The neglect of these exercises is the neglect of the spirit. The spirit withers when the exercises wane. Try these:

Practice his presence. Do not act "as if" he were present. Act because he "is" present. His nature and character both reveal his presence. He is as present as the air you breathe. Even the most brief touch with this reality as you start a day can give energy for any occasion. He will never leave you or forsake you. Never! Your feelings may deny this truth. Do not let your mind ignore it.

Search the Scriptures. Read the Word for yourself. It will amaze you what light the Bible throws on the Bible. Many persons spend a great deal of time reading *about* the Bible and little time reading it. Establish a systematic program of Bible study which includes daily memorization.

The Bible is God's language. Through it he is still speaking to people today. To understand a person it is essential to understand that person's language. Don't let the Bible be a foreign language to you.

Remember that not all books which contain Scriptures are scriptural. Often when a text is taken out of its setting it can be misapplied. The simplicity of the Scriptures is in this: when it is read and texts that speak to the same subject are compared, the topic becomes clear.

Don't take time to read the Bible. If you try to do that, you'll find you don't have time. Don't take time—make time. You are under orders. Don't neglect reading the assignment.

Pray. Don't let prayer become your last resort. Let it be your first resource. Avoid letting your prayer time become only an occasion when you inform God of what you want. Be sure it's not simply a time for lecturing the Lord, Be still and listen. Be open to change. Let God lead your thoughts through his Word to his will. This will enable you to do his work.

Prayers of praise are good therapy. They cleanse the mind and open your thoughts to the greatness of God. Such elevated thought will lift the spirit. It will make you aware of the resources available for daily combat. Praise him even when you don't feel like it. This indicates dependence on him, not depression from circumstances. If with your mind you will priase him, even when your emotions do not agree to it, you will soon find your feelings in concert with your faith. Praise is an act of the will, not of the emotions.

3. We Express

We have a God in which we "have our being." In Christ a person can have *completeness of personality.*

Hopefully this stage in your life is only the beginning of bigger and better things. A look at your future may enable you to see a horizon with much to offer. Yet, don't overlook today in your rush to reach tomorrow. Many persons crucify today on a cross between the two thieves of yesterday and tomorrow. Start where you are, with what you have. Just don't fail to start.

In retrospect a college professor said, "I have led a toothless life. I have never bitten off anything. I was saving myself for the future, for later on, and I have awakened to the fact that my teeth are gone." Give yourself now. With your whole heart confront today's challenge. Don't let "becoming" prevent your "being." The Scriptures speak of one's present, perpetual "being" in Christ.

Tagore wrote, "I have spent my days stringing and unstringing my instrument, while the song I came to sing remains unsung." Sing it while you can still hear the music. Be a doer, not a delayer, with an awareness of being in Christ ... venture. You can dare to be bold. This concept charges life with expectancy and courage.

Oliver Wendell Holmes commented, "Many people die with their music still in them. Why is this so? Too often it is because they are always getting ready to live. Before they know it time runs out."

Though there appears to be much sand in the hour glass of your life, realize it is running and will some day run out. So develop yourself to the fullest, starting now. Give your maximum one day at a time.

May the epitaph on your grave marker not read:

> He dined beneath the moon
> He basked beneath the sun.
> He lived a life of going to do,
> And died with nothing done.

See yourself as a person who lives and moves and has his being in the presence and because of the power of a loving God. Picture yourself as his beloved child he watches over. Realize he is allowing you to become a mature, developing total person. He has not offered to exempt you from problems. He has promised to be with you, to guide, and comfort you. Accept his promise and enjoy his presence.

See yourself as being as distinct among people as each snowflake is among all others. As unique as a leaf among all others. Never try to compare yourself to any other person. This relative exercise is never smart. You are the only original you. Don't try to copy anybody and thus commit suicide of personality and character. Be the you only you can be. Let the world catch a glimpse of a designer original—you.

See yourself as being in union with your Creator. See yourself as a part of his plan. Some youth become despondent when challenged with the question, "What difference do you make in the world?" Your influence on the total world may be minimum. For most persons this is true. But the only issue is, what impact will you have on your sphere of influence? The size of that sphere is not important. What goes on in it is. See yourself as in the realm of God's rule. Conquer your area for him. That concept can change conditions.

Realize you can overcome past failures and mistakes. The past can become, not just ancient history but nonexistent.

Your past can be buried in the grave of God's grace. Never again will there be a trace of any sin confessed. Your old defeated self-image can be discarded. You can start over. This is only the beginning.

Try these new concepts:

I can have an emotionally happy life.

I can do all things God intends for me to do because of his help.

I can face difficulties and even defeats without being defeated.

I can overcome my fears with faith

I can trust myself when under authority to God.

I can be the me that he intended me to be.

I can change.

I can . . .

A concept is an unhatched egg. Be sure you are sitting on a nest full of good ones. They are going to hatch, and your are going to have to live with them.

9. Happiness Is an Inside Job

"Hello! How are you doing?"

"Oh, pretty good, under the circumstances."

Under the circumstances? It seems many people live in this shadowy subterranean world. You can come out. It is possible to overcome circumstances and live above them.

Don't let circumstances dictate your disposition, development, or destination. It must be conceded they will either defeat you, or you will overcome them. Your strength and determination, not their impact, will decide which.

Most success stories are tales of struggles to overcome circumstances. Charles Spurgeon said, "Many men owe the grandeur of their lives to their tremendous difficulties."

Sir Walter Scott learned from lameness; George Washington, the patient statesman, from the snows of Valley Forge; Lincoln, the liberator, from his poverty; Disraeli, the crusader for fair play, from prejudices against him; Theodore Roosevelt, the disciplinarian, from his asthma; Edison, the inventor, from deafness; Chrysler, the creative inventor, from the grease pit of a locomotive roundhouse; Robert Lewis Stevenson, the poet of pathos, from tuberculosis; Walter Judd, the surgeon-statesman, from his acne and skin cancer; Helen Keller, the inspiring example, from her blindness, deafness, and muteness; Jane Needham, author of *Looking Up*, from her iron lung.

Beethoven's "Ninth Symphony," Handel's "Messiah," and Michelangelo's masterful Sistine Chapel paintings are all examples of victories over circumstances.

In each instance the circumstances seemed insurmountable. However, in each case the character was undeniable.

In a letter to a friend Martha Washington wrote: "I have learned too much of the vanity of human affairs to expect any felicity from public life. But I am determined to be cheerful and happy in whatever situation I may be. For I have also learned from experience that the greater part of our happiness or misery depends on our dispositions and not on our circumstances."

So now you are starting a new venture. You are going to see the world. It will be beautiful—if you want it to be. If you have a determined mind and a disposition to smell the roses, see the sunset, eat the savory fruit, and feel the kitten's fur, you have a thrilling time ahead. If you become preoccupied with the thorns, clouds, sticky fingers, and sharp claws, life is a jump without a chute.

Happiness is an inside job!

There is an ancient legend about a time when people abused wisdom. So a council of Wise men decided to take away the secret of success and happiness. Once agreed, then they had to decide where to hide it.

One of their number suggested digging deep into the center of the earth and burying it there. All others disagreed with, "Man's curiosity will prompt him to drill deep into the earth and find it."

Yet another suggested sinking it to the depth of the ocean floor. "No," came the answer, "man's adventurous nature will prompt him to plumb the depths and find it."

Still another urged that it be abandoned on the summit of the tallest mountain. "Absurd," the majority agreed, "eventually man will venture there and find it."

Finally the wisest of the wise men spoke, "Here is what

we will do with the secret of success and happiness. We will hide it deep inside of man himself, for he will never think to look for it there."

"Wonderful," the group shouted with glee, "that is the one place man will fail to search for it."

Success and happiness are not dependent on circumstances but upon one's determination and disposition.

Nothing holds people in bondage like an undisciplined mind. Nothing ever really sets a person free but self-control.

It is a marvelous achievement to be able to paint a beautiful picture. It is a noteworthy accomplishment to be able to carve a lovely statue. It is a far greater attainment to be able to color the atmosphere through which you look at life. Being able to mold events and affect the quality of a day is a much more significant accomplishment. Such is the highest of arts. You can become a master craftsman. It all comes from within.

Sir Francis Bacon said: "A wise man will make more opportunities than he finds." Don't wait for circumstances to give you a break. Never blame your failures on "bad luck." Go out and constructively make your luck. Extend yourself and make a break. You were not created to be a puppet dangling on the strings of circumstances. You have a free will and can affect circumstances. Circumstances are blind and mindless. You have creative powers. Think your way through. You can work and pray until you see clearly.

"Osmosis" is a word used to describe a chemical process. It can be illustrated by placing two solutions of water in a container and separating them only by a thin, porous cloth. Suppose one of these solutions to have a high-salt concentration, and the other to be distilled water. With the water being agitated only slightly, osmosis will occur. The solution of greater salt concentration will seep into the distilled water. The process is called osmosis. Always the greater concentration will influence the one of lesser.

You and circumstances are like that. The water had the capacity of moving in either direction through the cloth. The strength of the solution affected which way the flow was to go. If your determination and desire are stronger than circumstances, then you will control those circumstances. If the reverse is true, then they will control you.

An example of this is the Old Testament character, Job. Think of his circumstances. First note . . .

What the Devil Did to Him

There was devastation. All of Job's farm animals were killed, along with his camels, sheep, and most tragically, his family. His losses were personal and heavy. His emotions were extended just like those of anyone with like circumstances.

There was disease. From the top of his head to the bottoms of his feet he was covered with skin sores. The pain was so intense that it even felt good to scrape them with broken pottery. There was no relief. Every possible posture was uncomfortable. His suffering was horrid. He was wrestling with pain with no holds barred. Pain almost had him pinned. When the body is suffering from such extreme pain it is difficult to think straight.

There was doubt. His doubt was short-lived. It is understandable that, at least for a brief time, doubt strutted through the streets of his mind. When it does in your life and there are things difficult to understand, remember— God is always a good God. Make your interpretations in light of that unchanging reality. He is always a good God. Consider . . .

What His Friends Did to Him

They derided him. Critically they assumed the worst. They asked, "What have you done to deserve this?" Their assumption was false. Such a negative attitude on behalf of friends who become critics is depressing. Our society is given to such negative interpretations of events. People assume the worst. They anticipate evil as a cause of all things unpleasant. At a time when Job needed the support of his friends, they became his critics.

They deserted him. After staying around for a few days and asking critical questions, they walked out on him. Just when he needed them most, they deserted him. Friends can be a big source of strength. His source soured.

They depressed him. Even his wife urged him to curse God and die. Why not? He would have been better off in heaven. After all, in heaven there is no need for antihistamines, aspirin, bandages, sedatives, stimulants, antacids, or foot powder.

Does Job appear to be an enlarged image of you? Are you ever derided, deserted, or depressed? Have you ever suffered devastation, disease, or doubt? If so, Job may well be your prototype—your model.

Such were the circumstances under which Job found himself. His former health, wealth, friends, and family were all lost. Fate had dealt him a cruel, violent blow. He was knocked down—but not out.

Not only did the devil and friends create circumstances of a crisis nature, Job brought some very unpleasant things on himself. He also negatively affected his circumstances.

What Job Did to Himself

In the Book of Job, it is recorded that he said, "The thing which I greatly feared ..." (3:25). Job had a negative mindset. He was inclined mentally toward what actually came to pass.

Self-actualization plays a big part in all of life. For this reason the Scripture warns, "As he thinketh in his heart, so is he" (Prov. 23:7). Our thoughts often dictate actions.

We control circumstances only so far as we control ourselves. That control can be positive or negative. Think failure, and chances are very good you will not succeed. However, if you think success, chances are very good you will not fail. Your mind matters immensely.

Job was in a negative frame of mind when things caved in on him. He had a "I-told-me-so" complex.

Job acknowledged being afraid. He spoke of having "great fear." Of all liars, your fears are the worst.

Lightning has flashed fright into people for centuries. One man faced this age-old fear and made the force of electricity bow down and serve him. Through the ages, humankind feared the uncharted seas. Mankind found a new world once the fear was overcome. The oceans that shrouded continents from each other now serve as lanes of transportation. Look a fear in the eye and it will shy away. Otherwise it will become a tyrant to rule over you.

Who is more foolish, the child afraid of the dark or the man afraid of the light? It is the unknown that causes fear. Understanding dispels it. Job, at the time of his fear, didn't know the Lord like he later would after undergoing circumstances. Fear always springs from ignorance. Job was soon to test and find sufficient the grace of God.

Resolve to maintain a positive attitude, regardless of circumstances. An episode in the life of Sir Robert Scott reveals it can be done under extremely adverse conditions. He and two friends, Wilson and Bowers, were the last three survivors of their exploration to the South Pole. As their ultimate end became evident, Scott wrote in his diary a statement addressed to Wilson's wife: "I should like for you to know how splendid he was at the end—everlastingly cheerful and ready to sacrifice."

At that stage of their venture they were several miles from their next camp. All hope of reaching it had vanished. The temperature was 40° below zero at midday. Antarctica had been conquered. Their dream had been fulfilled as Scott made his last entry in his diary: "We are pegged out in a comfortless spot ... We are in a desperate state, being frozen. No fuel and a long way from food, but it would do your heart good in our tent to hear our songs and the cheery conversation. We are very near the end but have not and will not lose our good cheer. We could have come through had we neglected the sick. The great God has called me."

The conquest of Antarctica was trivial compared to their overcoming the circumstances. That was their real show of character. Their attitude evidenced they were not "under the circumstances." They had mastery of their lives' most miserable moment.

Conditions did not suggest that they should be of good cheer. Their character enabled them to have it. If history could testify on their behalf, it would probably reveal that their cheer under those circumstances was in character with all of their lives.

Plan in the good times your attitude for hours of adversity by practicing the right responses. Program your responses in the good times so your instincts will carry you through the bad.

Job was anxious. He acknowledged, "Neither had I rest." Anxiety, that is worry, is to life what sand is to the bearings of a perfect wheel. It irritates the nerves, clouds the mind, deadens sensitivity, and blinds logic. Energy is wasted, momentum lost, and dynamic depleted by worry.

A husband explaining to his wife why she was always tired described her like this: "You always do everything three times. First, you anxiously anticipate it, wondering if you can do it. Then you do it. Next, you worry about whether you did it right. You always do everything three times. No wonder you are always more tired than anyone—you are doing three times as much."

Job's nervous anxiety might well have conditioned him for what happened in his life.

To prevent clothes from sagging it is a good idea to remove all items from the pockets before hanging them. To prevent a sagging spirit, remove all burdens from your mind each night before going to bed. Take them out of your mind and place them on the altar before God in prayer. This can relieve your mind of its burdens. As the removal of items from the pockets prevent a garment from sagging, so the practice of prayer can avoid a sagging spirit.

It is not the work, but the worry,
    That drives all sleep away,
As we toss and turn and wonder
    About the cares of the day.
Do we think of the hands' hard labour,
    Or the steps of the tired feet?
Ah, no! but we plan and wonder
    How to make both ends meet.

It is not the work, but the worry,
    That makes us troubled and sad,
That makes us narrow and sordid
    When we should be cheery and glad.
There's a shadow before the sunlight,
    And ever a cloud in the blue,
The scent of the rose is tainted,
    The notes of the song are untrue.

It is not the work, but the worry,
    That makes the world grow old,
That numbers the years of its children
    Ere half their story is told;
That weakens their faith in heaven
    And the wisdom of God's great plan.
Ah! 'tis not the work, but the worry
    That breaks the heart of man.

                     —Anonymous

He was agitated. Job's expression, "yet trouble came," literally means, "agitation keeps coming back." He was recycling the same negative thoughts. The Lord can help you reprogram your mind. Worry is merely the projection of negative thoughts about future or past events. Never let your mind leave a topic of thought on which you have been thinking negatively. Discipline yourself to turn off the projector of your thought process and reload. Now, before leaving the subject, project a positive Bible concept on the subject. Make it a policy to practice this consciously until it becomes second nature. In this way you can train your mind to dispel doubt, fear, and pessimism. Flood it with faith, hope, and love. These positive attitudes can refresh the spirit.

What Was the Outcome?

Job prayed for his friends (Job 42:10). Friends? They had been the devil's instruments to deride, desert, and depress him. Now he responded to them. He did unto them what he needed them to do unto him.

Jesus Christ urges his followers to pray for those who persecute them. Why? Because he loves us and them. Prayer for oppressors flushes bitterness. This is good, for bitterness does more harm to the vessel where it is stored than to the person on which it is poured. Forgive! It may not have any constructive influence on the person forgiven, but it will on the forgiver. Realistically, the unforgiving are unforgiven because they are unforgivable.

This is a sure way to get on top of your circumstances. Don't work under the load of resentment and hostility. Job's reinstatement was not as a result of repentance (v. 6) but of his intercession (v. 8,9). As Job, pray for your accusers. This kind of love is the insignia of rank in eternity.

Job put his trust in God (13:15). Before his sufferings he knew God by reputation. He even argued with God. He accused God of malfeasance, that is, not fulfilling his duties (Job 10).

Job repented, that is, he had a change of mind about God (42:6). The three conclusions Job reached about God can help *anyone* come out on top under any circumstances. He observed:

"I know my redeemer liveth . . ."
　　Job had an awareness of God

"I know He knows me . . ."
　　Job knew God had an awareness of him.

"Yea, though he slay me yet will I trust in him . . ."
　　Job knew God was always a good God—worthy
　　of trust regardless of circumstances.

Job prospered (42:10). These gifts which he received after his faithful response to the circumstances were not a reward for his virtue. They were a gesture of God's grace.

Not all prosperity is material in nature. Often the gain is not visible. It is no less enjoyable, though. The knowledge that by God's grace you have overcome circumstances is fulfilling. It is so rewarding that it is worth taking a lifetime to accomplish.

Don't quit—now this is

only the beginning!

10. How to Wage Peace

"Tunnel vision" is a term used to describe an eye problem. It refers to a person who has no peripheral, that is, side vision. The field of view is limited. The term was coined because of what it represents. If you look through a tunnel, only that which is within the narrow limits of the other end can be seen. The scope of sight is restricted.

This same term can be applied to the way some people think. They have "tunnel vision." They can see things only from their vantage point. As a result, their understanding of life and acceptance of people are limited.

There is a term used in physics and applied in photography that illustrates the fact of differing viewpoints. The word is parallax. It refers to one's point of view.

Help yourself understand this. Extend your arm its full length. Hold up only your index finger. Close your left eye and look at the finger. Position it with regard to the background against which you are looking at it. Now, without moving the finger, close your right eye as you open your left one. Be careful not to move your index finger. Though the finger actually does not move, it appears to. Now repeat this procedure rapidly by alternately opening and closing your eyes. The finger looks as though it is moving, but in reality it is not. It is your changing point of view that varies.

Many conflicts occur as a consequence of two persons looking at the same set of facts from a different point of view. Try to live with both eyes open. Strive to see the other person's perspective. Look for his point of view. You may never see it, but you will see him better.

One may not agree with a person even when his point of view is realized. Though you may not understand his logic you can by it better understand the person. This reduces conflicts.

Every person should make it his business to gather new insights and ideas from sources other than the environment where he works and lives daily. Broaden the mouth of your tunnel. Don't fail to stretch your field of understanding, and thus let your mind become stagnant, narrow, and closed to other people and principles.

This should not suggest that you will always agree with them. Neither does it imply that their viewpoint is better than yours. It does indicate that conflicts can be limited by better understanding of people and differing principles. Such understanding may well make you more confident in your own ideals and ideas.

There is a principle which is a barrier against all understanding, it is proof against all logic; it never fails to keep a person in everlasting ignorance. This principle is contempt prior to examination, or a closed mind. Only a self-assured person is willing to explore an adversary's opinion.

Our limited field of reference may cause us to be suspicious of those whose experience is different from ours. Some years ago a Greenland Eskimo was taken on the American North Pole expedition. He was a valuable help. His familiarity with the cold world aided everyone in the party. Later as a reward, he was brought to New York City for a short visit. When he returned to his native village, he told of the wonders he had seen. He described the houses that rose in the face of the sky, of houses that moved (street cars), massive bridges, and artificial lights.

His fellow tribesmen listened in disbelief. This formerly

respected villager was dubbed "Sagdluk," meaning "the liar." Though he spoke truth, their frame of reference made them suspicious. Conflict resulted. He lived a life of disgrace. Long before his death his real name was even forgotten.

Learn to respect the verifiable experiences of others, even if they are totally contrary to anything you have known. Time and the character of the person may be the only conclusive proof possible.

The word "educate" has its roots in the Latin word *educo,* which means to develop from within; to educe; to draw out; to grow through the law of use. Academic degrees may or may not indicate education. The truly educated person draws wisdom for life out of his reason. Such enables one to understand his environment and those in it. Understanding can reduce conflicts.

In the realm of personal faith, always remember the final filter should be the Bible. If a subjective experience of a person ever conflicts with the objective truth of the Bible, the former can be known to be improper or untrue. The reference of the Written Record must always be given preference. The Christian experience is an objective faith. It is belief in the object, Christ. It is not a subjective faith. That is, what I, the subjective, can do or allegedly have done.

Weigh experiences by the Word. This needs to be taken a step further. It is not to be done in accordance with the experiences of persons in the Bible, but by what the Bible says should be your experience. Understanding can help prevent conflicts.

Strive to disagree without being disagreeable. When a conflict occurs, be quick to forgive. Hurry to seek reconciliation. Never hold a grudge.

Be aggressive in waging peace. Take the initiative in seeking to recycle friendships.

No person is so big that he will never need to say, "I'm sorry." No individual is so perfect that he will never need to say, "Forgive me, I was wrong." A person can be so little that he will never be willing to make those and other related apologies. Most persons who are willing to admit error are considered to be gracious, genuine, and understanding.

No friendship can exist,
No family function,
No business prosper,
No relationship last
    Without conflict
        resolved by
            forgiveness, reconciliation, and love.

A good technique in trying to resolve differences is the feel, felt, found concept. It involves the three steps:

"I know how you feel . . .
    I felt that way too . . .
        Until I found . . . "

In using this approach you relate to the other person and demonstrate understanding and empathy. Next you imply an awareness that his viewpoint has logic. The logic was once found to be so strong that you accepted it also. Finally, you share the counter logic which changed your mind. At this point you are free to express fully your opinion without making the disagreeing partner feel like he is thought to be defending a weak position.

Abraham Lincoln, a man of wisdom, paralleled some concepts for us. In doing so he focused attention on age-old ideologies which still struggle for supremacy.

You cannot bring about prosperity
    by discouraging thrift.

You cannot strengthen the weak
by weakening the strong.
You cannot help the wage earner
by pulling down the wage payer.
You cannot further the brotherhood of
man by encouraging class hatred.
You cannot help the poor
by destroying the rich.
You cannot keep out of trouble
by spending more than you earn.
You cannot build character and courage
by taking away man's initiative and independence.
You cannot help men permanently
by doing for them what they could
and should do for themselves.

From these and other key ideas, choose your beliefs. Once you have chosen them, be prepared for conflicts. Every point has a counterpoint. Any person who has an opinion can expect to encounter persons with opposing opinions. The only way to avoid conflict, of course, is never to have an opinion of your own.

Never for the sake of peace and quiet, both of which are admirable, deny your own convictions. As much as is within you, strive to live peaceably with all people, but not at the price of compromise. Never give up just to get out of conflict.

If it's true that part of the price paid for convictions is conflict, then it pays to be sure your convictions are worth defending. If you are going to stand for something, make sure it deserves your support.

Some conflict-reducing factors:

• Keep your voice down ... tone is as important as content.

- Demand of yourself that you listen with understanding.
- Train yourself to write legibly.
- Maintain your good humor.
- Manifest love toward the person advocating an opposing position.
- Always attack the problem, not the person.
- Decide: Is winning an argument worth losing a friend?
- Make sure your priorities are in order.
- Always try to leave open further relations for future friendship.
- Be aggressive in trying to recycle friendships.
- Avoid embarrassing others.
- Do not detract from a person's self-worth.

The Worst of Conflicts

Conflicts between persons are bad. Conflicts between groups are worse. Conflicts between nations are war. The worst conflict of all is not interpersonal but *inner*-personal. A conflict within the self is devastating. A conflict between what a person *is* and *what he professes to be* is distressful.

Inner conflict produces loneliness. When the real self is kept out of sight, the pretentious self has all the friends. The real self, when kept hidden, never comes out to enjoy relationships with others. Such a person, even if in company with many people, is never really known. Friendship comes from openness and self-revelation. When the true self is kept hidden by a false mask of pretense, it becomes lonely.

Many young people are very good at putting on and taking off masks at the right moment. They wear one mask around parents, another around authorities, and still another with different friends. All the time, the true self remains in isolation and becomes lonely.

This dual personality results in a dueling personality, a self that is constantly in combat with itself. The two selves engage in a contest to see which is the stronger. Each weakens the other until the one surviving is itself a weak personality. Such a person is a walking civil war, a committee always bound up by a tie vote, a snake with a devouring head at both ends.

When this internal conflict exists, the person can never rest. It demands constant vigilance in order to be able to change masks in a moment. Fear of being found out creates stress. The tension grows until a breaking point is reached.

In the life of a two-faced person there is no internal control. This reduces self-respect. Which mask to wear is determined by the company in which the wearer finds himself. From this perspective, externals are in control for a mask-wearer. Identity is lost, and with it goes self-confidence. Nervous tension develops and a quarreling temperament emerges.

Perpetual defense is required by a person who has inner conflicts. Each personality phase has to defend the other. There are even times that one has to deny the other's existence. Soon people begin to notice this and withdraw, leaving greater cause for loneliness.

A hunger for identity and integrity grows within the divided mind. Self-respect and confidence are totally lost. A lack of consistency causes a lifeless character.

Though external forces seem to control an individual caught in this pattern of behavior, only the person can reverse the process. The inward flow of external influences must be stopped from within. It is an inside job.

Thomas Edison was once elaborately introduced by a youthful admirer. The lengthy introduction ended with a reference to Edison as the inventor of the talking machine. Edison tactfully responded: "God invented the talking machine. I invented the one that can be turned off."

Each person must provide a control. It is a matter of the will. Divine help is available. We would do well to pray with the Psalmist, "Set a watch, O Lord, before my mouth; keep the door of my lips" (Ps. 141:3).

The inner action of God and man together can accomplish almost anything. Human strength and initiative alone are not enough. Pretentious uninvolvement will not work, either. Some persons use the latter by saying, "I am just going to let Jesus do it all." Bible examples abound of God/man action. Joshua blew the horn, and the Lord caused the walls to fall. "The sword of the Lord and of Gideon" prevailed in battle. Moses lifted the rod, and the waters of the sea parted. Paul said, "I can do all things," but he didn't stop there. He completed the partnership, " . . . through Christ who strengtheneth me."

An eternal, internal armistice can be won. Your improper self can be forced to abdicate and allow your better self to exist. Heavenly help is available to achieve the overthrow.

Will you be a hero or will you be a coward? In helping the new, unified you emerge, you might well make four lists:

• An elimination list. What personality traits would you like to eliminate? Be specific.

• A cultivation list. What are the traits you most admire in your own life? Be honest.

• An admiration list. What are the traits you most admire in other people? Be selective.

• An imitation list. What are some admirable traits in others you would like to develop in your own life? Be ambitious.

You can develop into a person fit for yourself to know. Then you will be a person others will want to know. By being known, you will lose much of your loneliness. The true you can be openly greeted by well-known friends.

It is exciting to visit the famous art galleries of Europe. Masterful works of art attract thousands of admirers. As I stood before the Mona Lisa in the Louvre, I too found her unusually appealing. But I also remembered that at the time of her creation, much like that of other classical works of art, she was not well-received. The financial worth was minimal. Popularity was not immediate. It took time. An ageless popularity now belongs to her.

Give yourself time. The traits you most admire in others were not acquired in an instant. Let yourself grow. Someday you may be surprised to hear someone say, "I'd like to be like you."

The Height of Conflict

You are going to be tried before three courts.

The court of self.

The court of others.

The court of God.

It is strange that the second of these creates greater pressure for many. There is a burning desire by most people to gain the approval of this court. Disapproval is considered disastrous.

Yet, the one that matters most is the latter. That court is of lasting consequence. Approval there insures a proper verdict in the court of self. Avoid conflict with the court of God.

No person ever breaks God's laws. Many individuals *break themselves* on God's laws. His spiritual laws are just as logical as the laws of nature. They are even better-known and more predictable. Still persons try to defy them. Today many people try to defy gravity by their own initiative. Experience has proven that it can't be done. Conflict with

God's standards should be avoided—experience has also proven they cannot be defied. Avoid the conflict and consequent disappointment.

Ambition for approval by the Lord gives a peace that passes understanding. "Thou wilt keep him in perfect peace, whose mind is stayed on thee" (Isa. 26:3).

Avoidance of spiritual conflict brings peace to the nervous system. Tension is reduced. Nerves are calmed. Anxiety is abated. The cessation of spiritual conflict proves that in God's will "is our peace."

Constructive Conflict

Don't resent the conflicts of life that can be identified as God's sandpaper. Some events are allowed, in his permissive will, that are intended to help make and mold our lives. Think of those lives that at first might have been thought of as prolonged disasters. In retrospect, it can be seen that a loving God who is always a good God was shaping and sharpening those persons.

A certain individual's mother died when he was a baby. He had very little formal schooling because of hardships. He ran for the legislature but was defeated. He entered business, but the practices of his worthless partner drove them into bankruptcy. He loved a girl dearly, but she died. He later married but had an unhappy marriage.

He served one term in Congress but was defeated in his bid for reelection. He worked to gain appointment to the United States Land Office, but he did not make it. He tried to be a lyceum lecturer but failed. He ran for the Senate but was defeated. He ran for the office of vice-president but was defeated. His name—Abraham Lincoln.

Lincoln lived with the hope that each stage of failure was only the beginning of something better—made better by conflict.

11. The Choice of a Lifetime

She was seventeen. It was a shame to see such a lovely face stained with tears. Her popularity was shown by her being chosen "class favorite." Leadership ability was indicated by her being elected a class officer and captain of the cheerleaders. Life looked good. The sun of success shone on her.

Now she sat there sobbing out her story. For several months she had been dating a special guy. They were going steady. People thought they were made for each other.

Suddenly life went into eclipse. She was four months pregnant. He was evasive. Gasping for breath she said, "I don't know why I did it." After offering her comfort and counsel, I commented, "I know why you did it."

"You do? Why?" she pleaded.

"You did it because a long time before you did it, you decided to do it. You decided by the books you read, the movies you went to, the stories you listened to, and the records you played. A long time before you did it you developed an attitude of consent. It was just a matter of time before you did it."

Hurt and angered at first, she withdrew. Then with a sigh of resignation she said, "Yor're right. I did. I dreamed it long before I did it."

She had been trapped by the major ambush of courtship. What is intended to be so constructive and beautiful had been misused. As such it was destructive. Destructive?

Yes, it had destroyed her youth. Soon she was to be snatched from the joys of youth and thrust into the responsibilities of motherhood. Many of her friendships were to be ended, a number of them simply by her own withdrawal. Her free spirit was destroyed by guilt and shame. Her relationship with her parents would never again be the same, regardless of how hard they tried—and they did.

An executive with the American space program was once asked, "When is the best time to make a decision?" Instantly he replied, "Before you have to." He then explained. "If you will notice, on each console in the control center is a large, black book. Before each mission we program every phase of the mission. We also program every potential variation that can occur. So if anything goes wrong we do not have to decide what to do under the emotion of the moment. We have decided before we have to and can immediately carry out our decision."

When is the best time to decide what your moral values will be? Before you have to! In this frame of reference one youth said, "Some time ago I made a pledge to God that with his help I would live a pure and clean life for him. I settled that issue once and for all. Now I do not have to make many decisions because I made that one. I try to enjoy each date as unto the Lord. I simply ask him to help me keep my pledge. Before every date I resolve to help my date have a good time, but I am not going to do anything to dishonor Christ."

She had made her decision before she had to. Under the emotion of any condition, all she had to do was live in accordance with her commitment. The pressure was off once the pledge was on.

In the next months and years you will enjoy new freedoms. Parental restraints will be removed. The limitations of home will not exist as they once did. The close circle of friends who might "tell" will be dissolved. Away from home there will be license to do whatever you want. The fact is, you will do what you really want.

The Old Testament teenager, Daniel, found himself in such a position. He was away from home and in an environment where his moral standards were unpopular and uncommon. The pressure was severe. There was even the threat of death. It is said of Daniel, "He purposed in his heart not to defile himself."

Why not? No one would ever have told. After all, it would have been the popular thing to do. Then, as now, people went along with the standards of society. "Don't make others feel uncomfortable. It might appear that you think you are better than they. Please don't offend them. Everybody's doing it. Don't be an odd-ball. Who wants to be a "triangle"—a square who is not all there?

That is something of the pressure Daniel faced. And you can expect much of the same. Be a Daniel. Dare to be different in the right way. Resolve now to be true to your better self—the you Christ intends you to be.

God's Word is plain about the issue:

> Shun immorality and all sexual looseness—flee from impurity [in thought, word or deed]. Any other sin which a man commits is one outside the body, but he who commits sexual immorality sins against his own body. Do you not know that your body is the temple—the very sanctuary—of the Holy Spirit who lives within you, whom you have received [as a gift] from God? You are not your own, you were bought for a price—purchased with a preciousness and paid for, made His own. So then, honor God and bring glory to Him in your *body*" (1 Cor. 6:18-20, AMP).

Your own apartment or a college dorm will give you

many occasions when you must have a "made-up" mind in order to abstain from lusts.

For this reason, the Bible uses a word related to such. It advocates that one "flee youthful lusts." The expression translated "flee" actually means run so fast that you kick up dust. Don't flirt with disaster. To abstain—flee. Another youthful Old Testament character, Joseph, ran so suddenly from an older married woman that she tore his cloak trying to hold on. He too had a made-up mind.

"There is nothing wrong with sex before marriage. It's just that our society has built up a bunch of old-fogy regulations we need to free ourselves of. Once you get your head together on it being OK, there's no problem." That subtle smokescreen is being used more and more. It is a plea for permissiveness.

The historical fact is: At no time or place, in even the most primitive stages of culture, have people been able to live without some form of restraints. Social scientists now say: There never has been a state of primitive promiscuity where sex life was simply spontaneous or was allowed to function with no pattern at all imposed by the group.

To claim that sex concepts are wrong because society regulates them is foolish. The regulations are not the cause of the problems we have with sex. The problems we have with sex are the cause of the regulations. By disregarding the regulations we are causing more problems. A principle problem is *emptiness*. In turn, many try to fill and fulfill this emptiness by more improper sexual activity. So the cycle feeds itself and more frustration results. And the cause is the effect, and the effect is the cause.

God's laws regarding sex are not intended to frustrate us but to free us. They are based on the fact that premarital sex can harm persons.

A leading medical journal reported that premarital sex

growing out of the "New Morality" has "greatly increased the number of young people in mental hospitals." Current lenient attitudes toward sex "have imposed stress on some college women severe enough to cause emotional breakdown." Sexual promiscuity is a source of emotional conflict. It leaves a blight on the emotional system.

Sexual promiscuity is not hurtful because it is forbidden. It is forbidden because it is hurtful.

The depth of love is not measured by the liberty taken, but by the responsibility shown. A good principle is: "If you love someone, you will be loyal to him no matter what the cost." This loyalty lifts relationships above the animal-pleasure level. The standard no longer is "I love *it,* but I love *you.*" Love waits for marriage in order to assume the responsibility of sexual relations.

Sex therapy, open marriages, and free love are some terms used for what the Bible calls "fornication" and "adultery." Advocates of these philosophies are finding they may sound good in theory, but in practice are blind alleys. They are based on the assumption that all sexual affairs can be detached and impersonal. In reality, they are not. Counselors are finding many broken lives resulting from one of the parties getting overly involved emotionally. Others are crushed by the idea of competition. The thought of reducing love to performance gets humiliating.

Love is a very responsible relationship. The expression "free love" is a contradiction in terms. If it is free, it isn't love. If it is love, it isn't free. True love is responsible and responsive. It is more than biological. Love never fails. It can outlast anything. This rules out one-night stands.

Often a date will say, "I love you," meaning, "I love me and want to use you." This use of the term is on the plane with, "I love grapes," meaning "grapes really do something to by taste buds." What it really means is, "I like the way grapes taste to me—what they do for me."

To truly say, "I love you," means, "I respect, admire, esteem, honor, reverence, and pay homage to your life-style." It means, "I love what you *embody*, not just your body."

"I can't live without you" is a danger signal. It is a form of blackmail. It indicates an immature and perhaps even a sick mind. It is a threat. It is not a compliment.

Love can always wait to give. Lust can never wait to get. Don't confuse the two.

Consider the potential price of promiscuity.

- It can result in public announcement and legal action.
- It results in shame if exposed.
- It steals purity and wholesomeness.
- It can severely hinder normal, satisfying sexual relations after marriage.
- It can cause long-lasting guilt feelings.
- It involves the risk of pregnancy, the creation of life with an eternal destiny.
- It may cause the premature death of an infant if abortion is the resort.
- It suggests the possibility of venereal disease.
- It may result in a premature and immature marriage forced by premarital pregnancy.
- It is a violation of God's plan for the exclusive use of sex within marriage.
- It destroys one's testimony for the Lord.

The idea of dating, growing in love, becoming engaged, marrying, and reproducing is exciting. In proper order these stages are each more fulfilling than the other. They are intended to be progressive. Any reversal of the order results in problems. Any suggestion regarding moving from step one to step five is an invitation to heartache. This is true even of the most liberated mind.

Lust has no morals, is greedy, self-seeking, and lacks understanding. It seeks immediate fulfillment, is demanding and deceptive.

Love, by way of contrast, is reasonable, considerate, patient, kind, and is always willing to wait.

Love is more powerful than lust. Love listens, laughs; is joyful, understanding, open, warm, and sober. It is always more concerned about the partner than self.

"Knowing a person in-depth" is a term often used by psychologists. It means to get so well-acquainted with a person that his moods, attitudes, feelings, desires, and reactions can be known and understood. This refreshing kind of relationship is meaningful. It enables you to draw the best out of another and reveal yourself more fully.

Courtship is the period when you single out persons one at a time to develop such identity. The more varied the relationships, the more a person can decide what is best matched with his own life-style. Courtship is a self-education. During courtship you learn more about yourself, what you like and dislike, as well as who you can identify with and who you can't. There is as much self-revelation in courtship as there is understanding of others.

Some things to look for during courtship are:

Appearance: Avoid extremes. Perfection in dress may be an indication of an ego trip. A sloppy dresser may be revealing a lack of self-respect. The qualities of neatness and cleanliness become increasingly important in marriage.

Beliefs: What compatibility is there between you regarding such major matters as God and country? Many other lesser matters are important, but, these are primary. Do you both hold similar loyalty to your nation? Do you share a mutually expressive Christian faith? Is your religion something you can talk about comfortably? Compatibility in these areas is vital.

Courtesy: People are attracted to individuals who are polite and kind. This is true because courtesy indicates that the feelings of another are considered. It is a form of thoughtfulness. Common courtesies show that a person has basic good manners. Such a person is easy to get along with. His smooth touch results in a velvet reaction.

Discipline: This reveals a person who is in control. A person who can't control self is not likely to be able to manage the affairs of two or more in marriage. A hot head burns everyone around. A bad temper indicates a will that is not self-contained. A well-disciplined individual is in control of appetite, diet, sex, and money. Such a person is likely to be a self-starter. This involves initiative. Without it one is unproductive.

Enthusiasm: Only highly motivated people are enthusiastic. They have an appetite for what there is to be done. They overcome obstacles, break down bearers, and achieve the impossible. They generate energy in others. The enthusiastic are the inspired. Every significant accomplishment is a monument to enthusiasm. Failure retreats before the gritty giant called enthusiasm. Indifference can be overcome only by enthusiasm. Enthusiasm is derived from two Greek words, *en* and *theos*. *En* means "in" and *theos* is the Greek word for "God." Literally, it means the God within; actually, being full of God.

Faith: Christian compatibility can't be taught any more clearly than in 2 Corinthians 6:14, 17, and 18 in *The Amplified Bible.*

> Do not be unequally yoked up with unbelievers—do not make mismated alliances with them, or come under a different yoke with them [inconsistent with your faith]. For what partnership have right

living and right standing with God with iniquity and lawlessness? Or how can light fellowship with darkness?

So, come out from among (unbelievers), and separate (sever) yourselves from them, says the Lord, and touch not [any] unclean thing; then I will receive you kindly and treat you with favor, and I will be a Father to you, and you shall be My sons and daughters, says the Lord Almighty.

A mutually compatible Christian faith is the only ingredient in our society capable of holding two persons together in a joyous relationship.

Courtship which can be and should be one of the most delighful times of life needs defined lines. It is one of the most important periods in a person's life. Regardless of the length, it is the basis by which all events in marriage are interpreted. If there is patience, understanding, chastity, faithfulness, protectiveness, and genuine concern in courtship, marriage has a good index for interpretation. If there is greed, lust, sexual promiscuity, impatience, indifference, and rudeness, the marriage is doomed before it begins.

"Toughness" in courtship may appear to be cute. In marriage it rapidly matures into indifference and often deteriorates into brutality.

"Sexy" in courtship may come across as desirable. In marriage it reveals itself to be egotistical and impossible to live up to.

Flippant attitudes in courtship harden into unconcern and coolness in marriage.

In the period of courtship the person who wanted so badly to go steady with you early in your relationship may be revealing a sense of insecurity. In marriage this becomes a burden. An insecure person early develops fears and suspicions.

Courtship should be a time of exploration. It has in many instances become merely a time of sexual exploitation. The exploration should not be physical but psychological. It should be a time to study personality types and traits and characteristics you have in common. It is a period to search for what personality features go best with your disposition.

If a couple gets physically involved early in a relationship, they become blinded by emotions. Youthful sexual stimulation deadens reason and puts logic to sleep. So when sex alone becomes the basis for mate selection, disappointment is inevitable.

After marriage, every marriage, sexual drives begin to cool some. Later in marriage, every marriage, physical attractiveness declines. The marriage based on these qualities alone is doomed. The great American swindle has been to make people believe that sex alone is a basis for life together. Though it is a vital, intended part of a husband/wife relationship, it alone cannot sustain any marriage.

Going steady at a young age is a disadvantage. It is wise to date a variety of personality types in your search for the right one. Settling on one too soon leaves curiosity unanswered and potential unexplored. There might be some other personality traits you have not yet observed that may be more ideally suited to you. Look for them.

To avoid getting sexually involved, avoid familiarity. Do not put yourself in a position to compromise. You have only one set of emotions and glands. Different things stimulate and activate them. Often a fine, religious couple may be deceived by them. For example, they might attend a religious concert together and be stimulated by it. They may be moved with compassion and tenderness. If upon leaving they go some place alone, these noble emotions can deteriorate. Compassion may become passion. Spiritual love may suddenly be misunderstood and misapplied as physical sex. Avoid the possibility of compromise.

There is a way out for the person who has become too involved with the wrong person. Doubtless such a person has enough imagination to have considered how good life could have been with their "special someone." If that one is not the right one by God's standard, there is still hope. If a believer will break such a relationship, hope will survive.

First a break should be made in a mature, considerate manner. If it is to be a break, make it clean, clear, and reassuring of the personhood of the one being dropped.

Now center your like in Christ. Submit all of your life to his will. Ask him to help you in mate selection. Commit your courtship to him.

Reflect on how good you invisioned life to have been with the former friend. With your life centered in Christ it can be even better with the one he guides you to. Believe it! There is no way to lose with God's guidance. Even if you remain single all of your life and your life is centered in him, it will be fulfilling and meaningful. Celibacy for some is a gift of God. When it is, it is rewarding and gratifying.

Sex should be spoken of as sexual appetite rather than sexual drive. An appetite can be cultivated or curbed. Courtship is a time to curb it. Marriage is the time to cultivate it.

Realizing this, many young couples are now practicing presexual marriage; that is, they precede sex with marriage.

The everybody-is-doing-it syndrome is just an excuse for promiscuity. What if they are? Does that alone make it right? The issue is not "thus saith the gang." For those whose god is the gang, it does make it right. For those whose God is the Lord Christ, the issue is "Thus saith the Lord."

12. To Find the Unknown . . .
(Start with the Known)

An algebra teacher had just finished writing a very complicated problem on the chalkboard. It was so long that it covered practically the entire board. It was one of those that begins with 10 x plus and continued with several adding, subtracting, multiplying and dividing factors. At the conclusion, she posed this statement, "Find X." One not-so-bright, but very clever, student was asked to go to the board and find "x." He drew an arrow from the top of the board to "X" and wrote across the top, "There it is."

Some of life's complications are not so easily resolved. But algebra illustrates one basic principle in trying to find God's will. To find the unknown, always start with the known. There is no other way. If a student were to ignore the known in trying to solve a problem, he could never find the answer. Unfortunately, in the spiritual realm many try to ignore completely that part of God's will that is known, while professing to be looking for the unknown. It does not work. God only reveals his unknown will to those who are doing his known will. Why should he reveal more for a person not to do? When there is faithfulness in doing the known, then he graciously reveals more that it might also be done.

If you will do his will as you know it, you will know his will that you might do it. God has willfully put himself under obligation to lead his children. He has voluntarily committed himself to empowering and enabling his children to do his will.

There are some *common misconceptions* regarding God's will. These are better known than many truths pertaining to his will. Some are:

God's will is always hard to find. This is not true. Much of his will is distinctly spelled out in the Bible. Some is known through simple logic. At other times he allows the believer to use the basic tool of reason to apply principles he has stated in the Scripture.

God's will is always unpleasant. Some persons feel that God always has something unpleasant for his children. The beauty of his loving will is that he never once asks us to do anything that is not for our good. He never asks us *not* to do a thing other than for our good. Not to do his will is to engage in that which keeps you from the good he has in mind for you.

God's will is only for "professionals." God has a loving will for every person. His will is no less related to one person than another. Persons engaged in church-related vocations should be there because it is His will. Those engaged in what is commonly and improperly called "secular" occupations should be there because it is God's will for them. Every engagement should be considered sacred and none secular. God has a loving, perfect will for you.

Some who contend that they want to know God and do his will want only part of him. They want his blessings, but not his correcting. They want his help, but not his direction; his peace, power, comfort, and joy, but not that part of him that is surgical. They desire his benefits and blessings, but not his requirements. They seek his reason and rewards, but not his responsibilities.

Those who make knowing God and his will a work of art paint the most beautiful lifescapes. In your quiet times and private moments with him in prayer, ask for his guidance. By searching the Scriptures, you will head into life with the best credentials possible.

If a person is to experience divine guidance, there must be an expressed need and desire for it. Those who do not want to know his will in matters other than salvation have little chance of having it revealed to them. To know God's will . . .

State Your Commitment

If one is to experience divine guidance, there must be an acknowledged willingness to obey it. If one does not respect what a friend has entrusted to him, he cannot expect that friend to trust him with more.

If one is to experience divine guidance, it should not ever be expected to conflict with the Bible in any way. Personal impressions and Bible insight never conflict without the first being wrong. Always accept as correct the written record, regardless of how sincere a belief contrary to it might be. A common mistake is in thinking that divine guidance comes only through the abnormal. In our era with the Bible completed, God uses the extraordinary less and less. Thus, he is allowing us to walk by faith in the written facts rather than by feelings. The less one feels the need for abnormal signs, the better able he is to follow the leadership of the indwelling Holy Spirit in applying the written Word.

When (a) the written Word, and (b) the inward urge, and (c) the outward circumstances all blend as one, divine guidance is soon to be known.

Two biblical examples illustrate different responses by God regarding divine guidance. Gideon was called on by the Lord to deliver his people from the Midianite oppression. Gideon sought divine confirmation of God's will and got it. When King Saul went to war against the Philistines, he received no guidance from the Lord.

Why did God reveal his will to Gideon and leave Saul groping in the darkness of uncertainty?

Saul had asked for divine guidance, but he did it in a rebellious state of mind. Saul had not done God's known will in the past. At his wit's end he tried to use God without being willing for God to use him.

Gideon was eager to know and ambitious to do God's will. As with Gideon, so with all of His children, God longs to unveil his will to anyone who is willing to follow his instructions. This is confirmed by John 7:17, "If any man will do his will, he shall know of the doctrine."

Do not expect to know God's will so you can sit back and decide whether or not to do it. God will ambitiously guide his committed children, even in the little issues of life.

Perhaps many Christians find themselves in a position like I have discovered myself in. Oftentimes I pray: "Lord, I am doing what I am because, as best I know, it is your will. The only reason I am doing it is because, in light of what I know, I believe it to be your will. If I am doing the wrong thing, please forgive me and guide me because it is being done out of ignorance, and not obstinance toward your will."

To know God's will . . .

Start with the Known

Most believers know to do more than they are doing. So take a brief inventory of some things we know to be God's will and honestly ask yourself if you are doing them.

You know that it is his will for you to be saved. Your salvation is his will. He is, ". . . not willing that any should perish, but that all should come to repentance" (2 Pet. 3:9).

To receive this salvation one needs to turn from self-serving sin to serving the Savior as Lord. It is a matter of putting confidence in Christ. It results from trusting God to do what he says and proving a will to do what he asks. Faith *in* involves a commitment *to* Christ. He who abandons himself to God will never be abandoned by God.

Don't seek any other facet of God's will without first settling this most important part of his divine will. To neglect or reject it is to show an unwillingness to do what he wills most strongly for you to do.

Your sanctification" is his will.

"For this is the will of God, even your sanctification" (1 Thess. 4:3).

The Bible word, sanctification, has nothing to do with sinless perfection. Basically, it means "set aside for designated use." In the Bible days, places, objects, and people were sanctified. That is, they were set aside for designated use. It had nothing to do with sinlessness but with service. Regardless of your occupation, you are personally set aside for God's use. It is his will for you to be.

If you are to be a plumber, let your life flow with the Living Water.

If you are going to be an electrician, let your life show forth the Light of the World.

If you are going to be a judge or lawyer, pattern your life after the Just Judge of Eternity.

If you are to be a doctor or nurse, demonstrate your devotion to the Great Physician.

If you want to be a farmer or engage in agribusiness, model your life after the Lord of the Harvest.

If you are to be a teacher, let the Master Teacher be your example.

If you are to be a carpenter, builder, or architect, follow the pattern of the Master Builder.

Whatever you are to be or do, be sure you are set aside in that engagement for his use.

Your proper sexuality is his will.

"That ye should abstain from fornication: That every

one of you should know how to possess his vessel in sanctification and honour" (1 Thess. 4:3,4).

Social codes change, mores vary, but God's Word is
consistent regarding sexual morality. One's sexual potency
reaches a peak in young adulthood. Physical maturity often
motivates persons to experiment sexually. Sex is more than
the involvement of two bodies. It is a gift of God and is to be
set aside for use as he has instructed. The proper limitations
he has prescribed for its use are only and exclusively within
the realm of marriage. Pre-and/or extra-marital sex is improper. The Word of God advocates only presexual marriage, not premarital sex. Any violation of this standard is
mutiny against God. Any abuse of this intended use keeps
one from being his best self.

Biologically, almost any two persons can engage in
sensually stimulating sex. Though the result can be physically satisfying, it is never spiritually gratifying as God intended it to be.

If doing God's will is your intended desire, then sexual
sanctification is a must. Remember, one must do the known
in order to discover the unknown. Pretending to seek God's
will while engaging in sexual immorality would be foolish.
Be sure your sex life is set aside for use as God desires.

Your subjection to authority is his will.

Through the inspired penman, God instructs his children to be subject to authority (1 Pet. 2:13-15). It is impossible for a person to maintain obedient subjection to God and
manifest disobedience to lesser authorities which God has
established. A rebellious nature usually relates to all of life. If
one under proper authority to another is called on by that
authority to do what is contrary to God's will, then the Highest Authority should be obeyed. In doing so, the person
should realize that he is subject to the resultant displeasure
of the lesser authority. This is often the price of obedience.

This brings up the point that even when doing God's will, difficulty is often encountered. By doing God's will, Daniel was sentenced to the lion's den. Moses was following God's guidance when he came to the oasis, Miraba, and found it dry. Christ was surely acting in the will of the Father when he went to the cross.

In each instance of obedience, there was anticipation followed by frustration. The stories do not end, however, with the lion's den, a dry oasis, and an occupied tomb. Anticipation and frustration were followed by realization. The mouths of lions were closed, the dry rock flowed with water, and the tomb was left empty by the resurrection. The will of God, as known, was done in each instance. Blessings resulted even amid difficulties.

A chain of responsibility runs all through life. Every person is under authority. The person over you is under someone. Chase that to its ultimate, and even the highest earthly authority is under the authority of God.

Your faithful stewardship is his will. It is required of a steward that he be faithful. The word, *stewardship,* is of Anglo-Saxon origin. It came from the term, *sty-ward.* A *sty* was a pigpen. A *ward* was one who was in charge. So a *sty-ward* was one given charge of a pigpen. The word form and meaning changed. Now, it refers to all for which a person is responsible. It matters little how much one has; it matters greatly how one handles what is in his "ward."

An expression for this same thing is property management. Strive to use what is in your possession. Being faithful with even that which is least does not guarantee you will gain more. It will insure that you get the maximum out of what you have.

In matters of appearance, do the best you can with what you have, for goodness sake. You are not responsible for how you look. You are accountable for how you *appear.*

Good grooming is an indication of self-respect. It also hints of regard for others.

In the area of the academic, always extend yourself. If you are a "C" student, be the best "C" student you can. The same is true of "B" and "A." Exercise your mind. Memorize challenging passages. The mind, like a muscle, must be flexed. It becomes trustworthy when trusted and dependable when depended upon. Push back the frontiers of your knowledge all the days of your life.

In the arena of attitude, be a good steward. An attitude is more important than a fact. A fact cannot be changed; an attitude can. Maintain a good attitude at all times, at all cost. What you think about what happens to you affects what happens to you. You are what you think. You think what you are.

Your proper praise of God is his will for you.

"In everything give thanks: for this is the will of God in Christ Jesus concerning you" (1 Thess. 5:18).

A lack of thanksgiving is the first step in the terrible march of barbarism. Thanksgiving has no relationship to circumstances.

Thanksgiving is a response of submission. It is an acknowledgment of our gratitude *to* someone, not *for* something. It is a recognition that the Lord is God. Grace before meals means: "I gratefully submit to the hand that feeds me." Paul's statement should encourage us. He said, "I have learned. ..." In old age he acknowledged he had learned to give thanks. He did not do it instinctively, but he did learn to do it. Start now and cultivate the art.

Thanksgiving is a reaction of joy. Thanks is verbal. Giving is visual. A doctor does not judge the condition of a patient by his speech but by life's vital signs. So God does not just go by our words but by our lives. Fire can be found in the marsh, flowers in the snow, and fresh water springs in the salty sea. So joy can be found amid deep trouble.

Thanksgiving is a release of praise. Praise goes beyond understanding. Just as there is no ultimate number, so there is always a question mark standing at the end of the road. Praise changes it to an exclamation. The psalmist (22:3) recorded that God himself inhabited the praise of Israel. That means God is at home in the midst of people who praise him. A study of the Psalms will reveal that the author was often lifted from a state of despair by exercising a spirit of praise and thanksgiving. Thanksgiving is the oxygen of prayer. It enlivens and energizes it.

To find God's will. . . .

Sustain Your Search

Consistency in conduct is a refreshing gem in a wasteland. A persistent pursuit of purpose is profitable. God guides "completely."

He will give guidance for every area of life. God expects persons to use their own minds. Do not exhaust the Holy Spirit to the point of calling into question your own powers of logic and the commands of the Bible. Do not misuse the Holy Spirit as an excuse for failing to respond responsibly and rationally. Think! God guides "continuously."

He guides one step at a time. His leading is not sporadic. Being led by the Spirit does not mean getting a free ride. The Bible speaks of persons being "led" by the Spirit. The Greek word translated "led" is *ago*. It does not mean to draw or drag a passive weight. It does refer to leading an active agent to a desired goal. It is not like pulling a sled, but like guiding a horse. You are the agent who must move, but the Spirit is the influence who will guide. God guides "conditionally."

His leadership is conditioned on our precommitment to

follow. "Thy will be done" . . . results in his will being revealed. He does not lead those who will not follow. God guides "compassionately."

It is somewhat incorrect simply to speak of "the will of God." This is more easily illustrated than explained.

Take the son of a doctor. His dad desires for him to be a doctor, also. This is his father's *intentional* will. As the boy grows he expresses his desire to be a doctor. Then his expressed will is the same as his dad's.

The young doctor is drafted. His father is understanding. Under the circumstances, he wants his son to comply with the law. Induction into the military results in the young man's doing the *circumstantial* will of his dad. At this state he fully intends someday to return and go to medical school.

While in the military he meets an influential friend. They devise what they feel will be a very lucrative business scheme. The young man writes his dad and explains. He no longer desires to go to medical school. His new ambition involves a get-rich idea. Again the dad is understanding and explains his ambition for his son, but consents for him to explore. Now the young man is doing his father's *permissive* will.

After a short time, it becomes evident that the business venture is not going to work. The young man writes his dad to explain and says he wants to change his plan and go to medical school. His father is thrilled. Now the young man is doing his father's *ultimate* will.

Every person is engaged in God's will. God's intentional and/or ultimate will is always best. Do it—and you will find this is . . .

ONLY THE BEGINNING!